# GEMSTONES

# GEMSTONES

## CALLY HALL

*Photography by*
HARRY TAYLOR
*(The Natural History Museum)*

*Editorial Consultant*
DR. ROGER HARDING

A Dorling Kindersley Book

LONDON, NEW YORK, MUNICH,
MELBOURNE, and DELHI

**Project Editor** Alison Edmonds
**Project Art Editor** Alison Shackleton
**Series Editor** Jonathan Metcalf
**Series Art Editor** Spencer Holbrook
**Production Controller** Caroline Webber

First published in Great Britain in 1994
Reprinted with corrections in 2000
by Dorling Kindersley Limited
80 Strand, London WC2R ORL

A Penguin Company

A CIP catalogue record for this book is available from the British Library.

ISBN 0-7513-2731-X

Computer page make-up by Adam Moore

Text film output by
The Right Type, Great Britain

Reproduced by Colourscan, Singapore

Printed and bound by
South China Printing Company in China

see our complete catalogue at
**www.dk.com**

# CONTENTS

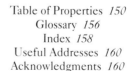

# AUTHOR'S INTRODUCTION

*The mysterious appeal of gemstones, their exquisite colours, and the play of light within them, would alone have made them precious to many, but their rarity, hardness, and durability have made them doubly valuable. The natural beauty, strength, and resilience of gems have inspired beliefs in their supernatural origins and magical powers, and stones that have survived the centuries have gathered a wealth of history and romance around them.*

THERE ARE OVER 3,000 different minerals, but only about 50 are commonly used as gemstones. Others are cut for collectors of the unusual, but are often not suitable for wear because they are too soft and easily scratched. In fact, the number of minerals regarded as gemstones constantly changes, as new sources and varieties are found and fashions change. Over 130 gem species, including some exceptionally rare stones, are described in this book, illustrating the very wide range of naturally occurring gemstones.

SORTING SAPPHIRES
*Workers in Burma sort through sapphires collected from river sediment. When cut, they epitomize the allure of gemstones – beautiful, rare, and durable.*

WHAT IS A GEMSTONE?

To be regarded as a gemstone, a mineral (or occasionally an organic material) must be beautiful, most importantly in its colour.

RIVER PEARL
(UNCUT)

STAR SAPPHIRE (CABOCHON)

DIAMOND (BRILLIANT-CUT)

FIVE MAJOR GEMSTONES
*These five stones are the most highly prized. All except pearl have a particular "cut" (shown in brackets) that brings out their best qualities.*

RUBY (STEP-CUT)

EMERALD
(OCTAGONAL CABOCHON)

A gemstone must also be durable – hard enough to survive constant use or handling without becoming scratched or damaged. Finally, it must be rare, because its very scarcity endows it with a greater market value.

### THE SCIENCE OF GEMMOLOGY

Gems are scientifically fascinating, too. Gemmologists make a complete study of each stone, both as it is found in rocks and after it has been cut and polished. That is why the species entries in this book show the gem in its rough, natural state, perhaps still embedded in the host rock (or "matrix"), as well as after it has

### EMBLEMS OF POWER
*The Cullinan I diamond (above), adorns the Royal Sceptre of the British Crown Jewels (right).*

been cut, polished, or carved. Many entries also feature a micro-photograph which reveals the internal structure of the stone by magnifying it many times. In this world within a world the gemmologist may turn detective, being able to distinguish between two outwardly similar stones, or between a natural stone and a fake.

### KINGS AND COMMONERS

Throughout the ages, gemstones have been seen as representations of wealth and power. Symbols of supremacy, from crowns to richly decorated robes, have traditionally been adorned with jewels. But

### PRIVATE COLLECTION
*The Mathews collection in London comprises 4 boxes of unmounted gems from all around the world (above), and a group of Colombian emeralds (right). The scope of this collection is unique, but many fine examples of cut and uncut gemstones are on public display in museums.*

gemstones are not just for the wealthy or the scientifically minded: they can be appreciated by anyone, from the amateur gem-spotter to the enthusiast who enjoys their beauty and history. For this reason, the *Gemstones Eyewitness Handbook* is not intended as a textbook, but as a general introduction and an initial guide to identification.

## COLLECTING GEMS

For many, the real satisfaction comes from actually owning gems. Most people cannot afford the more

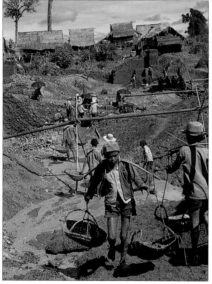

MINING IN CAMBODIA
*In many parts of the world, traditional methods and equipment are still employed for the collection of gemstones.*

expensive stones, but anybody can collect a few minerals that, even if not gem-quality, are still very attractive. You may even chance on a piece of amber on a beach, or come across a beautiful piece of jewellery in a local auction. No matter how modest your collection, it will give you hours of fascination and enjoyment.

A BOX OF JEWELS
*In the 18th century, jewelled trinkets like this decorative box were very fashionable. A large, citrine is in the centre, surrounded by amethyst, agates, amazonite, garnet, and pearls.*

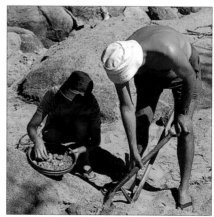

FOSSICKING IN AUSTRALIA
*Fossicking (foraging) for sapphires and opals is still possible in parts of Australia, as long as you first obtain a permit from the authorities. River beds and streams are the best locations.*

# How This Book Works

THIS BOOK is divided into three parts: precious metals, cut stones, and organics. Cut stones are arranged by crystal structure into seven groups (cubic, tetragonal, hexagonal, trigonal, orthorhombic, monoclinic, and triclinic), but with a final section on amorphous gems. Within these sections, gem species are grouped with other species of a similar mineralogical type. The page below explains a typical entry.

crystal group to which gem belongs •

basic chemical composition of gem •

mean hardness of gem, measured on Mohs' scale •

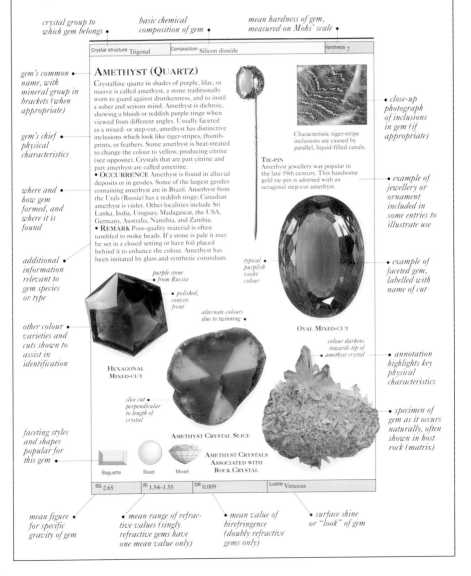

Crystal structure Trigonal | Composition Silicon dioxide | Hardness 7

gem's common • name, with mineral group in brackets (when appropriate)

gem's chief • physical characteristics

where and • how gem formed, and where it is found

additional • information relevant to gem species or type

other colour • varieties and cuts shown to assist in identification

faceting styles • and shapes popular for this gem

## AMETHYST (QUARTZ)

Crystalline quartz in shades of purple, lilac, or mauve is called amethyst, a stone traditionally worn to guard against drunkenness, and to instil a sober and serious mind. Amethyst is dichroic, showing a bluish or reddish purple tinge when viewed from different angles. Usually faceted as a mixed- or step-cut, amethyst has distinctive inclusions which look like tiger-stripes, thumb-prints, or feathers. Some amethyst is heat-treated to change the colour to yellow, producing citrine (see opposite). Crystals that are part citrine and part amethyst are called ametrine.
• OCCURRENCE Amethyst is found in alluvial deposits or in geodes. Some of the largest geodes containing amethyst are in Brazil. Amethyst from the Urals (Russia) has a reddish tinge; Canadian amethyst is violet. Other localities include Sri Lanka, India, Uruguay, Madagascar, the USA, Germany, Australia, Namibia, and Zambia.
• REMARK Poor-quality material is often tumbled to make beads. If a stone is pale it may be set in a closed setting or have foil placed behind it to enhance the colour. Amethyst has been imitated by glass and synthetic corundum.

Characteristic tiger-stripe inclusions are caused by parallel, liquid-filled canals.

• close-up photograph of inclusions in gem (if appropriate)

TIE-PIN
Amethyst jewellery was popular in the late 19th century. This handsome gold tie-pin is adorned with an octagonal step-cut amethyst.

• example of jewellery or ornament included in some entries to illustrate use

purple stone • from Russia

• polished, convex front

alternate colours due to twinning •

typical • purplish violet colour

• example of faceted gem, labelled with name of cut

OVAL MIXED-CUT

colour darkens towards tip of • amethyst crystal

• annotation highlights key physical characteristics

HEXAGONAL MIXED-CUT

slice cut • perpendicular to length of crystal

AMETHYST CRYSTAL SLICE

AMETHYST CRYSTALS ASSOCIATED WITH ROCK CRYSTAL

• specimen of gem as it occurs naturally, often shown in host rock (matrix)

Baguette | Bead | Mixed

SG 2.65 | RI 1.54–1.55 | DR 0.009 | Lustre Vitreous

mean figure • for specific gravity of gem

• mean range of refrac-tive values (singly refractive gems have one mean value only)

• mean value of birefringence (doubly refractive gems only)

• surface shine or "look" of gem

# WHAT ARE GEMSTONES?

GEMSTONES are generally minerals that have been, or may be, fashioned to use for personal adornment. As a rule, they are beautiful, rare, and durable. Most are minerals: natural, inorganic materials with a fixed chemical composition and regular internal structure.

A few gems, like amber and pearl, come from plants or animals, and are known as organics. Others, called synthetics, do not have a natural origin, but are made in laboratories. They have very similar physical properties to natural gems, and may be cut to imitate the real thing.

## PRECIOUS METALS

The precious metals are gold, silver, and platinum. They are not true gemstones, but they are attractive and easily worked, often as settings for gems, and have their own intrinsic value. Platinum is the rarest and the most valuable.

POLISHED STONE
*Crystals may be rounded and polished naturally (like this emerald pebble, rolled in a stream), or ground mechanically.*

GOLD RING

GOLD NUGGET
(UNWORKED)

## ORGANICS

Gem materials produced by living organisms are called "organic". Their sources are as diverse as shellfish (which produce pearls), polyps (whose skeletal remains form coral), and the fossilized resin of trees (which makes amber). Ivory, jet, and shell are also organics. These materials are not stones, and are not as durable as mineral gems. Instead of being cut in facets like mineral gems, they are usually polished or carved, or drilled and threaded as beads.

NATURAL CRYSTAL
*In its natural state the mineral may be a prism, with clearly defined faces.*

## CUT STONES

Like the emerald shown here, almost all cut gems begin life in a crystalline form (see pp.18–19), embedded in a host rock known as the matrix. In this state, the stone is referred to as "rough". Many natural crystals are attractive enough to be displayed as they are. Others are faceted and polished to enhance their beauty (see pp.26–29), then set in a piece of jewellery or an ornament.

AMBER BEAD

AMBER ROUGH

## CABOCHON
*A simple fashion for stones is to cut them* en cabochon, *producing a domed, highly polished surface.*

## FACETED STONE
*Most gemstones are cut to give them a number of flat surfaces, called facets. The facets absorb and reflect light, to magical effect.*

## IMITATION EMERALD
(GARNET ON GLASS)

## IMITATIONS
Gemstones have been imitated throughout the ages. Many lesser stones have been used, as well as glass paste and other man-made materials. Composite stones, like the red garnet on green glass (above), are made of more than one piece.

## JEWELLERY
*A piece of jewellery, usually one or several polished or faceted stones set in a mount of precious metal, is often the finished product.*

## SYNTHETICS
Man-made, synthetic stones (see pp.34–35) are similar in chemical composition and optical properties to their natural equivalents. In the flux method, crystals are grown, then faceted (right).

SYNTHETIC
CRYSTALS

SYNTHETIC
FACETED EMERALD

# HOW GEMSTONES ARE FORMED

Gemstones that have a mineral origin are found in rocks, or in gem gravels derived from these rocks. Rocks themselves are made up of one or more minerals, and may be divided into three main types. The formation of these three types – igneous, sedimentary, or metamorphic – is a continuous process, best described in terms of the rock cycle (shown right). Gem-quality minerals within these rocks may be easily accessible at the Earth's surface, or lie buried deep beneath it. Others, separated from their host rock by erosion, are carried by rivers to lakes or the sea.

IGNEOUS ROCKS
*form as molten rock solidifies, above or below ground. This erodes and is deposited as sediments.*

• SEDIMENTARY ROCKS
*are formed from the accumulation and compression of eroded rock fragments. They may eventually be buried back below the surface.*

• METAMORPHIC ROCKS
*may be either sedimentary or igneous rocks whose character is fundamentally changed by heat and pressure.*

*peridot crystals form as lava cools* •

VOLCANIC BOMB FORMED FROM BASALTIC LAVA

## IGNEOUS ROCKS

Igneous rocks have solidified from molten rock, which comes from deep beneath the Earth's surface. Some, called "extrusive" igneous rocks, are thrown out from volcanoes as lava, volcanic bombs (see left), or ash. "Intrusive" igneous rocks are those that solidify beneath the surface. Essentially, the slower a rock cools and solidifies, the larger the crystals – and therefore the gemstones – formed within it. Many large gemstone crystals form in a kind of intrusive igneous rock known as pegmatite.

## METAMORPHIC ROCKS

Metamorphic rocks are either igneous or sedimentary rocks that have been changed by heat and pressure within the Earth to form new rocks with new minerals. As this happens, gemstones can grow within them. Garnets, for example, form in rocks called mica schists, which were once mudstones and clays. Marble, formed from limestone that has been subjected to intense pressure and high temperatures, may contain rubies.

*kyanite and staurolite crystals form under high pressure* •

KYANITE-STAUROLITE SCHIST

## SEDIMENTARY ROCKS

Sedimentary rocks are formed by the accumulation of rock fragments produced by weathering. In time, these fragments settle down and harden into rock once more. Sedimentary rocks are usually laid down in layers, and these may be shown as a feature in decorative stones. Most Australian opal occurs in sedimentary rocks; turquoise occurs mainly as veins in sedimentary rocks such as shale; halite and gypsum *are* sedimentary rocks.

• blue-green opal in veins and fissures

**AUSTRALIAN OPAL IN SEDIMENTARY ROCK**

## ORGANIC GEMS

Organic gems come from plants and animals. Natural pearls form around foreign bodies that have made their way inside the shells of marine or freshwater shellfish. Cultured pearls are produced artificially in large fisheries, many in the shallow waters off the shores of Japan and China. Shells treated as gems may come from animals as diverse as snails and turtles, living in the ocean, in fresh water, or on land. Coral is made up of the skeletons of tiny marine animals called coral polyps. Bone, or ivory from the teeth or tusks of mammals, may come from recently living animals or from fossils thousands of years old. Amber is fossilized tree resin, collected from soft sediments or the sea. Jet is fossilized wood, found in some sedimentary rocks.

TREASURE FROM THE SEA
*The action of sea water has given this piece of amber (fossilized tree resin), washed up on a beach in Norfolk, England, a pitted and worn surface.*

MODERN DIAMOND MINE IN BOTSWANA
*Some gemstones are so valuable that large-scale mining, in which tonnes of rock may be extracted to collect tiny amounts of gemstone, are still viable.*

ALLUVIAL MINING FOR SAPPHIRES
*Small-scale mining with traditional methods and equipment, such as this in Sierra Leone, is still common in many under-developed countries.*

# WHERE GEMSTONES ARE FOUND

SOME GEM MINERALS, such as quartz and garnet, are found worldwide. Others, like diamonds and emeralds, are rarer, due to the more unusual geological conditions necessary for their formation. Even when a mineral is found worldwide, only a minute proportion may be of gem quality. The main gem localities of the world are therefore those where gem-quality material occurs in sufficient quantity to make production economic.

## DIAMONDS OF AFRICA
*The kimberlite rocks of southern Africa are mined in a modern, large-scale way, producing vast quantities of diamonds for both industrial and gem use.*

*United States*

*Mexico*

*Germany* •

*Italy* •

*Niger*

*Colombia*

*Brazil*

*Zambia*

*Botswana*

*South Africa*

## KEY TO SYMBOLS

| | | | |
|---|---|---|---|
| DIAMOND | RUBY | SAPPHIRE | EMERALD |
| AQUAMARINE | CHRYSOBERYL | TOPAZ | TOURMALINE |
| PERIDOT | GARNET | PEARL | OPAL |

## TWELVE KEY GEMS
*The 12 varieties of gemstone shown on this map represent some of the world's best-known gems. All are popular and highly prized, but some are far rarer than others.*

## PEARLS IN JAPAN
*The shallow coastal waters of the Japanese islands offer ideal conditions for farming pearl oysters. Pearls are organic gems, and therefore independent of geological conditions.*

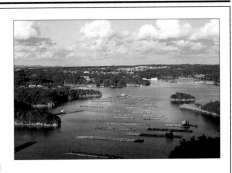

Russia

Former Czechoslovakia

Afghanistan

China

Japan

Egypt

Pakistan

Burma

India

Thailand

Zaire

Sri Lanka

East Africa

Madagascar

Australia

## WORLD DISTRIBUTION
This map shows the main localities for 12 key gems. Each gem may of course occur in other places, but probably not in sufficient quantities to make its extraction economic. Some sites, although historically important, may now be worked out.

## RUBIES IN BURMA
*The rich mineral deposits of Mogok in Burma have yielded some of the world's finest rubies, although extraction is by traditional methods. Sapphires are also mined here.*

# PHYSICAL PROPERTIES

THE PHYSICAL PROPERTIES of gemstones, their hardness, their specific gravity or density, and the way they break or "cleave", depend on chemical bonding and the atomic structure within the stone. For example, diamond is the hardest natural material known, and graphite is one of the softest, yet both are made of the same element, carbon. It is the way in which the carbon atoms are bonded together in diamond that gives it a greater hardness and resilience.

### HARDNESS
One of the key qualities of a gemstone, hardness may be measured by how well a stone resists scratching. Every stone can be tested and classified using the Mohs' scale of hardness (below), which gives every mineral a figure from one to ten. Intervals between numbers on the scale are not equal, most obviously between nine and ten (see the Knoop scale, right). Hardness testing is destructive, however, and should only be used on a gemstone if other tests fail.

**TESTERS**
*The point of each of these testing pencils is one of Mohs' minerals.*

### KNOOP SCALE
*This scale shows the indentation caused by a diamond point when it meets the surface of a mineral. The 10 stages correspond to Mohs' points.*

### MOHS' SCALE OF HARDNESS
*The Mohs' scale was devised by the German mineralogist Friedrich Mohs as a means of classifying the relative hardness of minerals. He took ten common minerals and put them in order of "scratchability": each one will scratch those below it on the scale, but will be scratched by those above it.*

MOHS' MINERALS

| 1 | 2 | 3 | 4 | 5 | 6 | 7 | 8 | 9 | 10 |
|---|---|---|---|---|---|---|---|---|---|
| TALC | GYPSUM | CALCITE | FLUORITE | APATITE | ORTHOCLASE | QUARTZ | TOPAZ | CORUNDUM | DIAMOND |

### SPECIFIC GRAVITY
The specific gravity (SG) of a gem is an indication of its density. It is calculated by comparing the stone's weight with the weight of an equal volume of water. The greater a stone's specific gravity, the heavier it will feel. For example, a small cube of pyrite, with an SG of 5.2, will feel heavier than a larger piece of fluorite with an SG of 3.18; and a ruby (SG 4.00) will feel heavier than an emerald (SG 2.71) of similar size.

PYRITE

**RELATIVE WEIGHTS**
*The smaller piece of pyrite (SG 5.2) feels heavier than the fluorite (SG 3.18), because it is more dense.*

FLUORITE

## CLEAVAGE AND FRACTURE

Gemstones may break in two ways: they either cleave or they fracture. Which way they break depends on the internal atomic structure of the stone. Gems that cleave tend to break along planes of weak atomic bonding (cleavage planes). These planes are usually parallel, perpendicular, or diagonal to the crystal faces (as both planes and faces are directly related to the stone's atomic structure). A gemstone may have one or more directions of cleavage, which may be defined as perfect (almost perfectly smooth), distinct, or indistinct (examples are shown right). Gems with perfect cleavage include diamond, fluorite, spodumene, topaz, and calcite.

When a gemstone breaks along a surface that is *not* related to its internal atomic structure, it is said to fracture. Fracture surfaces are generally uneven, and each type has its own descriptive name, shown in the examples below and right.

**BARYTE**

**◁ PERFECT CLEAVAGE**
*Fragile baryte has three directions of easy cleavage, giving smooth surfaces.*

**ALBITE**

**△ DISTINCT CLEAVAGE**
*Although not perfectly smooth, albite's cleavage surfaces can be clearly seen.*

**◁ INDISTINCT CLEAVAGE**
*Cleavage direction is indistinct in aquamarine.*

**DUMORTIERITE**

**△ UNEVEN FRACTURE**
*An uneven fracture surface is typical of fine-grained or massive gems like dumortierite.*

**AQUAMARINE**

**OBSIDIAN**

**△ CONCHOIDAL FRACTURE**
*The type most commonly found in gemstones, the name refers to the shell-like fracture surface.*

**GOLD**

**HACKLY FRACTURE △**
*Rough, uneven fracture surface, seen on the right of this gold specimen.*

**NEPHRITE**

**SPLINTERY ▷ FRACTURE**
*Interlocking texture causes splintery fracture.*

# CRYSTAL SHAPES

MOST MINERAL GEMSTONES are crystalline, with their atoms arranged in regular and symmetrical patterns, like a lattice; a few are amorphous, with no or only a weak crystal structure. Crystalline minerals may consist of a single crystal, or of many in a group. Polycrystalline minerals are made up of many, usually small, crystals; in cryptocrystalline minerals the crystals are too small to see without the aid of a microscope.

Crystalline minerals are made up of a number of flat surfaces called faces; the orientation of these faces defines the overall shape, which is known as the "habit". Some minerals have a single, characteristic habit, such as pyramidal or prismatic; others may have several. A lump of crystalline mineral without a definite habit is called massive. Amorphous gemstones, like obsidian and tektites, have an irregular shape. Examples of common habits are shown right.

this natural glass cooled too fast for crystals to form

**AMORPHOUS**

some crystals form with a characteristic pyramidal end •

**PYRAMIDAL**

rutile needles in this rock crystal have an acicular habit

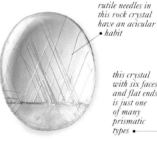

this crystal with six faces and flat ends is just one of many prismatic types •

**ACICULAR (NEEDLE-LIKE)**

**PRISMATIC**

## TWINNING

Natural crystals are seldom perfect. Their growth is influenced by external factors such as temperature, pressure, space, and the medium in which they grow. One irregularity that may occur is known as "twinning" – when the internal structure of the crystal is repeated. Twins grow together in a number of different ways.

• twinned crystals may show alternate colours

**TWINNED AMETHYST**

• irregularly shaped mass with no apparent crystal habit

**MASSIVE**

crystal • habit is branch-like

**DENDRITIC**

# CRYSTAL SYSTEMS

Crystals are classified into seven different systems, according to the "minimum symmetry" of their faces. This depends on a crystal's "axes of symmetry" – imaginary lines (shown in black in the artworks on this page) around which a crystal may rotate and still show identical aspects. The number of times the same aspect may be seen – in one 360-degree rotation around an axis – defines that axis as two-fold, three-fold, etc., up to six.

**PYRITE**

**CUBIC**
*Crystals in the cubic system (also known as the isometric system) have the highest symmetry, e.g. cubes, octahedra, and pentagonal dodecahedra. The minimum symmetry is four three-fold axes.*

**HEXAGONAL/ TRIGONAL**
*These systems (thought by some to be one system) share the same axis of symmetry. Hexagonal crystals have six-fold symmetry; trigonal crystals three-fold.*

**MILKY QUARTZ**

**TETRAGONAL**
*This system is defined by one four-fold axis. Typical crystal shapes include four-sided prisms and pyramids, trapezohedra, and eight-sided pyramids.*

**ZIRCON**

**MONOCLINIC**
*The monoclinic system has a minimum symmetry of one two-fold axis. Prisms with basal pinacoids are common crystal shapes found in this system.*

**TOPAZ**

**ORTHORHOMBIC**
*The minimum symmetry of this system is three two-fold axes. Typical crystal shapes are rhombic prisms and pyramids with basal pinacoids, and rhombic double pyramids.*

**BRAZILIANITE**

**TRICLINIC**
*Triclinic crystals have no axis of symmetry, so gemstones within this system are the least symmetrical.*

**AXINITE**

# OPTICAL PROPERTIES

COLOUR IS THE MOST OBVIOUS visual feature of a gem, but in fact it is just one of many optical properties, all of which are dependent upon light. The individual crystalline structure of a gemstone (see pp.18–19), interacts with light in a unique way, and determines the optical properties of each gem species. Effects produced by light passing *through* a gem are described here; those produced by the *reflection* of light are described on pages 22–23.

## WHAT MAKES COLOUR?
The colour of a gem depends largely on the way it absorbs light. White light is made up of the colours of the rainbow (spectral colours), and when it strikes a gem some spectral colours are "preferentially absorbed". Those that are not absorbed, pass through or are reflected back, giving the gem its colour. Each gem in fact has a unique colour "fingerprint" (known as its absorption spectrum), but this is only visible when viewed with a spectroscope (see p.38). To the naked eye, many gems look the same colour.

SPLITTING LIGHT THROUGH A PRISM
*Splitting white light into its spectral colours is called dispersion, and gives gems their internal fire.*

## ALLOCHROMATIC GEMS
Allochromatic ("other-coloured") gems are coloured by trace elements or other impurities that are not an essential part of their chemical composition. Corundum, for example, is colourless when pure, but impurities in it (usually a metal oxide) create the red stones we know as rubies, blue, green, and yellow sapphires, and orange-pink padparadscha. Allochromatic gems are often susceptible to colour enhancement or change.

RUBY (RED CORUNDUM)

PURE CORUNDUM

SAPPHIRE (BLUE CORUNDUM)

## IDIOCHROMATIC GEMS
The colour of idiochromatic ("self-coloured") gems comes from elements that are an essential part of their chemical composition. Thus idiochromatic gems generally have only one colour, or show only a narrow range of colours. Peridot, for example, is always green, because the colour is derived from one of its essential constituents, iron.

PERIDOT

PERIDOT

## PARTI-COLOURED GEMS

A crystal that consists of different-coloured parts is called parti-coloured. It may be made up of two colours (bicoloured), three (tricoloured), or more. The colour may be distributed unevenly within the crystal, or in zones associated with growth. The many different varieties of tourmaline probably show the best examples of parti-colouring, exhibiting as many as 15 different colours or shades within a single crystal.

*bicoloured crystals can make attractive gemstones; junctions of colour zones may be distinct (as • here) or gradual*

**WATERMELON TOURMALINE**

## PLEOCHROIC GEMS

Gems that appear one colour from one direction, but exhibit one or more other shades or colours when viewed from different directions, are known as pleochroic. Amorphous or cubic stones show one colour only; tetragonal, hexagonal, or trigonal stones show two colours (dichroic); orthorhombic, monoclinic, or triclinic stones may show three colours (trichroic).

**IOLITE (BLUE ASPECT)**

*iolite is strongly pleochroic: colourless from one direction; blue when • rotated 90 degrees*

**IOLITE (COLOURLESS ASPECT)**

## REFRACTIVE INDEX (RI)

When a ray of light meets the surface of a polished gemstone, some light is reflected, but most passes in. Because the gem has a different optical density from air, the light slows down and is bent from its original path (refracted). The amount of refraction within a gem is called its refractive index (RI) and, with the DR (below), can be used to help identify the stone.

*calcite is highly birefringent, producing double • images*

**CALCITE**

**SEEING DOUBLE**
*Zircon's back facets look doubled, due to strong double refraction (DR).*

### BIREFRINGENCE (DR)

*When viewed through a refractometer (far right), cubic minerals like spinel are singly refractive, showing a single shadow edge; doubly refractive minerals like tourmaline split light rays in two, producing two shadow edges. The difference between the two gives the "birefringence" (DR).*

**SPINEL**

**TOUR-MALINE**

## LUSTRE

The overall appearance of a gemstone, its "lustre", is determined by the way light is reflected from its surface. This is related to the degree of surface polish, which is generally greater the harder the stone is. Gemmologists use a variety of terms to describe lustre and its degree of intensity. "Splendent" means that the stone reflects light like a mirror; but if little light is reflected, the lustre may be described as "earthy" or "dull". Stones with a lustre comparable to diamond are described as "adamantine", and are the most desirable. In fact, most transparent, faceted gems have a glass-like, "vitreous" lustre; the precious metals have a "metallic" lustre; and organic gems show a range, from "resinous" to "pearly" and "waxy". Some gemstone species vary in their lustre: garnets, for example, range from the resinous hessonite garnet to the adamantine lustre of demantoid garnet. Rough lazulite and howlite have a dull, earthy lustre, which is vitreous after polishing.

*hematite crystals, like pyrite and the precious metals, • display metallic lustre*

**METALLIC LUSTRE**

*hard and highly polished, the look of a diamond defines • adamantine lustre*

*the glass-like lustre of this ruby is the most • common for cut stones*

**ADAMANTINE LUSTRE**

**VITREOUS LUSTRE**

*waxy lustre is most commonly associated with • turquoise*

*• the greasy lustre of this polished imperial jadeite is comparatively rare*

**WAXY LUSTRE**

**GREASY LUSTRE**

*organic • gems, like this amber bead, may occur in a range of lustres, depending on the nature of the material*

*satin spar gypsum is commonly cited to describe silky lustre •*

**RESINOUS LUSTRE**

**SILKY LUSTRE**

# INTERFERENCE

Interference is an optical property caused by the reflection of light off structures within a gemstone. This internal reflection gives a play of colour. In some stones it will produce the full range of the spectral colours; in others just one colour may predominate. In opal, interference occurs because of the structure of the stone itself – spheres arranged in regular three-dimensional patterns. This produces the rainbow effect called iridescence, also shown by a number of other gems such as hematite, labradorite, and iris quartz. In moonstone feldspar, interference at the junctions of its internal layers (thin, alternating layers of different types of feldspar) produces a shimmering effect just below the surface of the stone, known as adular-escence, opalescence, or a schiller (sheen).

moonstone feldspar exhibits a bluish white shimmer or sheen

**ADULARESCENCE**

**LIGHT LAYERS**
*Iridescence appears at layers within labradorite.*

light reflected from labradorite gives a rainbow effect

**IRIDESCENCE**

hematite shows a play of colour

blue and green may predominate within opal

**IRIDESCENCE**

**IRIDESCENCE**

# CAT'S-EYES AND STARS

When a gemstone is cut *en cabochon* (with a domed, polished surface), light reflecting from the stone's internal features, such as cavities, or fibrous or needle-like inclusions (see pp.24–25), may create a cat's-eye effect (chatoyancy) or star stones (asterism). One set of parallel fibres gives rise to the cat's-eye effect; two sets of fibres produce a four-rayed star, three sets of fibres a six-rayed star, and so on.

reflection from acicular (needle-like) rutile crystals gives a six-rayed star

**SAPPHIRE STAR STONE**

parallel fibres within the stone produce the cat's-eye "flash"

**CHRYSOBERYL CAT'S-EYE**

# NATURAL INCLUSIONS

INCLUSIONS ARE INTERNAL features of gems. They may be solids, liquids, or gases that the crystal enclosed as it grew, or cleavages, cracks, and fractures that filled (or partly filled) after the host material finished growing. Although usually regarded as flaws, inclusions today are often seen as adding interest to a stone. They can also be invaluable in identifying a gem, because some are peculiar to a particular species, while others occur only in a particular locality.

## FORMATION OF INCLUSIONS

Solid inclusions have usually formed before the host stone – the crystals of the host have grown around them and enclosed them. They may be distinct crystals or amorphous masses. Solids and liquid inclusions formed at the same time as the host are aligned to its atomic structure. For instance, the stars in star rubies and sapphires are caused by needle-like crystals of rutile, which formed parallel to the crystal faces at the same time as the host corundum crystals. Cavities filled or fractures healed after the formation of the host give inclusions that resemble feathers, insect wings, or fingerprints.

MICROSCOPE
*A microscope that magnifies between 10 and 40 times is one of the most useful instruments for examing inclusions in gemstones.*

• *stone-holder to allow viewing from any angle*

DIAMOND WITH GARNET
*Solid inclusions may be the same gem type as the host, or different – like the garnet in this diamond.*

PERIDOT "WATER LILY" (MAGNIFIED 30 TIMES)
*Inclusions that look like water lily leaves are a typical feature of peridot from Arizona, USA. They consist of a central chromite crystal surrounded by liquid droplets.*

## MOONSTONE "CENTIPEDES"
*These insect-like inclusions (magnified 35 times) are a common feature of moonstone. In fact they are parallel cracks caused by strain.*

## INSECT IN AMBER
*Insects are sometimes found trapped in amber, caught by the sticky resin as it was exuded. Insects have been added to some imitation amber to create a natural effect.*

## RUTILE NEEDLES
*This carved rock crystal perfume bottle contains inclusions of needle-like rutile crystals. Tourmaline and gold are also found in rock crystal.*

## ALMANDINE GARNET (ABOVE)
*Magnified 45 times, the grey patch on the left is a rounded apatite inclusion. The bright interference colours to the right are due to a zircon crystal.*

## EMERALD (LEFT)
*Rectangular cavities with tails (magnified 40 times) are sometimes found in natural Indian emeralds.*

# FACETING

THE MOST USUAL METHOD of fashioning a gem is to cut the surface into a number of flat faces, known as facets. This gives the stone its final shape, or "cut". The craftsman, or lapidary, who cuts the stone aims to show its best features, taking into account its colour, clarity, and weight. He may, however, have to compromise to retain weight and therefore value. The blue diagrams on the opposite page show the most popular cuts, and are used throughout the book.

## HOW A STONE IS FACETED

There are several stages in the cutting of a gemstone, each of which may be carried out by a different expert. In our example, a rough diamond crystal is fashioned into a brilliant-cut. This is the most popular cut for this stone because it maximizes the gem's naturally strong light dispersion. However, because each stone is a different shape, or has imperfections within it, or because retaining the weight is of paramount importance, the cut in its ideal form (the "make") may not be possible. Nevertheless, the essential aim is to make the diamond bright and "sparkling", showing flashes of colour called fire. To this end, the size, number, and angles of the facets are mathematically calculated. The rough crystal is sawn or cleaved to obtain a basic workable piece, then turned on a lathe against another diamond to give it a round shape. The facets are then cut and polished in stages, and the stone is given a final polish before mounting.

**1. ROUGH**
*A rough diamond crystal is selected for faceting.*

**2. CUT**
*The top is cut off, and the stone rounded on a lathe by another diamond.*

crown •
bezel •
• girdle

**3. GRIND**
*The central facet – the flat table – is ground first, then the bezel facets.*

table
• facet

**4. TOP AND BOTTOM**
*More facets are put on in groups and in sequence: the star facets and upper girdle facets on the crown; then the lower girdle facets and the culet on the pavilion (the underside).*

• bezel facet

upper girdle facet •

**5. FINISHING**
*A "brillianteer" then adds a further 24 facets above the girdle and 16 below.*

• star facet

**6. MOUNTING**
*After a final polish, the stone is mounted in precious metal.*

## BRILLIANT-CUTS
The brilliant-cut is the most popular for diamonds, and for many other stones, particularly colourless ones. It ensures that maximum light is reflected out through the front, giving brightness and fire. Variations in the outline give the oval, the pear-shaped pendeloque, and the boat-shaped marquise or navette.

**BRILLIANT-CUT SAPPHIRE**

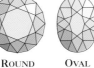

**ROUND**        **OVAL**

**RINGS OF FIRE**
*These gold rings from the house of Cartier are set with diamonds, sapphires, rubies, and emeralds, in a mixture of cuts from brilliant to fancy.*

## STEP-CUTS
The step-cut (or trap-cut) shows coloured stones to advantage, having a rectangular or square table facet and girdle, with parallel rectangular facets. The corners of fragile gems may be removed, making octagonal stones – as, for example, in most emeralds.

**OCTAGONAL STEP-CUT SPESSARTINE**

**TABLE**        **SQUARE**        **OCTAGONAL**

**BAGUETTE**        **OVAL**

## MIXED-CUTS
Mixed-cut stones are usually rounded in outline, with the crowns (above the girdle) cut as brilliants, and the pavilions (below the girdle) step-cut. Sapphires, rubies, and most transparent coloured stones are cut in this style.

## FANCY-CUTS
These have several possible outlines, such as triangular, kite-shaped, lozenge-shaped, pentagonal, or hexagonal. The cut may be used for rare gems, or to make the most of a flawed or irregularly shaped gem.

**FANCY-CUT HELIODORE**

**CUSHION**

**MIXED**

**MIXED-CUT PERIDOT**

  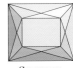

**PENDELOQUE**   **MARQUISE**   **SCISSORS**

# POLISHING, CARVING, AND ENGRAVING

PRECIOUS METALS AND GEMS – usually massive, microcrystalline stones and organics – can be worked by polishing, carving, or engraving. Polishing is the oldest form of fashioning. Carving produces three-dimensional objects by cutting them from a larger mass of material. Engraved images are made by scratching out lines or holes, or by cutting away to leave a raised image. Carving and engraving require tools harder than the material being worked.

## POLISHING

The shine given to the surface of a stone – either by rubbing it with grit or powder, or against another stone – is its polish. Dark-coloured gemstones and those that are translucent or opaque, for instance opal and turquoise, are often polished rather than faceted, as are organic gems. They may be polished as beads or as flat pieces to be used in inlay work, or cut *en cabochon* with a smooth, rounded surface and usually a highly polished domed top and flat base.

drum contains
abrasive grits and
polishing powders •

### PEBBLE POLISHER
*Gem fragments of similar hardness may be turned into attractive pebbles (left) by tumbling in a drum containing abrasive grits and polishing powders (right).*

**MOTOR-DRIVEN TUMBLING DRUM FOR POLISHING**

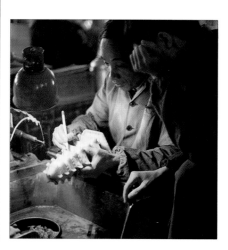

## CARVING
Carving usually refers to the cutting of decorative objects from a larger mass. Stones as hard as 7 on the Mohs' scale were carved in Ancient Egypt, Babylonia, and China. Impure corundum (emery) was used for carving and engraving in India; nowadays a hand-held chisel or turning machine is used. Popular stones for carving include serpentine, Blue John, malachite, azurite, rhodonite, and rhodochrosite.

### CHINESE CARVING
*Carving of gemstones in China dates back to the Neolithic period. The most prized material was imported nephrite jade, and decorative objects like this model pagoda are still made.*

## ENGRAVING

Engraving usually refers to the decoration of the surface of a gemstone by the excavation (scratching out) of lines, holes, or trenches with a sharp instrument, known as a graver or turin. Of all engraved objects, cameos and intaglios are perhaps the most popular. A cameo is a design (often a human profile) in flat relief, around which the background has been cut away. In an intaglio it is the subject, not the background, that is cut away, creating a negative image that may be used as a seal in clay or wax. Intaglios were particularly popular with the Ancient Greeks and Romans, and are still prized by collectors.

### GOLD ENGRAVING
*The surface of gold and other precious metals used in jewellery may be decorated with intricate patterns, using a hand-held chisel called a graver.*

Engraved gemstones gained prominence in Europe in the Renaissance period. During the Elizabethan period in Britain cameo portraits were often given as gifts, particularly among the nobility. All through the ages, layered stones have been used for cameos or intaglios, with onyx and sardonyx particularly popular. Other gems suitable for engraving include rock crystal, amethyst, citrine, beryl, peridot, garnet, lapis lazuli, and hematite, as well as organic materials such as ivory and jet.

*• pearl bead*

*chrysoberyl •
cabochon*

### BEAD
*Spherical gems such as pearls may be pierced and threaded as beads on necklaces.*

### CABOCHON
*This simple cut is used to display colours and optical effects in opaque and translucent stones.*

*moonstone
• cameo*

*lapis •
lazuli
polished
slab*

### CARVING
*The cameo symbol used in this book is intended to denote both carvings and engravings.*

### POLISHED STONE
*Decorative stones given a flat, polished surface may be used in ornaments and jewellery.*

### MODERN DESIGNS
*This citrine prism, with its clean, architectural lines and exquisite engraving, demonstrates the flair and craftmanship of modern designers. Its maker, Bernd Munsteiner, uses conventional cuts to create classic modern jewels akin to pieces of sculpture. Bernd Munsteiner is one of many artists working in Idar-Oberstein in Germany. Together with Hong Kong, Idar-Oberstein is considered to be one of the most important centres for carving and engraving gemstones today.*

**ENGRAVED CITRINE**

# GEMS THROUGH THE AGES

PEOPLE EVERYWHERE, throughout history, have followed a natural instinct to collect things of beauty and value, and have used whatever gems they found locally – from shells to sapphires – to adorn themselves. Today, the whole range of the world's gems is available to those who can afford them. There are more gem-producing areas than ever before, new stones are on the market, and jewellery designs continue to evolve. But the inherent attraction of gems – their beauty, durability, and rarity – remains the same.

## FIRST USES

Gem materials were probably first used as much for their durability as their beauty. But beauty was not ignored, even then. For example, the Stone Age obsidian axe below has been wrought to be attractive as well as practical, and ancient civilizations did fashion gems purely for adornment. Although most were primitive in design, some were highly intricate, with painted surfaces. Down the ages, gems have also been offered as prestigious gifts, and their portability and intrinsic value gave them a natural use as currency.

### QUARTZ BEADS
*The pebbles in this necklace from Ghana were once used as a form of currency.*

## EARLY COLLECTORS

The earliest collectors found gems with no more equipment than a stick or shovel, a basket, and a sharp eye. Similar Stone Age tools found in the Mogok area of Burma show that rubies have been mined there for thousands of years – and the same methods of panning the stream with wicker baskets are used today. Evidence of more organized early mining – for example, abandoned mines and waste dumps – is found in the Urals of Russia, on the shores of the Mediterranean, in Cornwall, England, and in many other places worldwide.

### OBSIDIAN AXE
*A natural volcanic glass, obsidian could be fashioned into a razor-sharp tool or weapon.*

### EMERALD IN LIMESTONE
*Emerald has been sought after for many thousands of years, the earliest known mines dating back to Egypt, 2000BC.*

## ANCIENT JEWELLERY

Very little jewellery made before the 18th century survives. The best examples are probably those of Ancient Egypt, much of it gold set with gems such as turquoise, lapis lazuli, and carnelian. It shows the great skill of the Egyptian goldsmiths: the gold refined, annealed, and soldered; the gems fashioned – probably using silica sand, a technique also known to the Ancient Chinese. The Romans went on to develop the polished stone rather than the setting. The art of the goldsmith and lapidary survived in the Dark Ages, though in medieval times gothic style was functional – mainly buckles, clasps, and rings.

### CLOTHED IN JEWELS
*Civilizations through the ages have used jewellery for adornment. This late 18th-century miniature shows an Indian woman clothed in richly jewelled necklaces, earrings, bracelets, and amulets.*

### MERMAN
*In this typical 16th-century pendant, a pearl forms the torso, with diamonds and rubies set in gold around it.*

## UP TO THE PRESENT

With the discovery of the Americas in the 15th century, European trade in gemstones expanded, and 16th- and 17th-century jewellers could use gems from all over the world. With the rise of an affluent merchant class, jewellery became more widely owned, and diamonds first became fashionable. In the 20th century, an increase in demand for affordable gems, and the scarcity of the most valuable, will doubtless continue the trend to use more varied gem species in jewellery.

### GEM-ENCRUSTED MODERN BROOCH
*Jewellery has passed through many styles, from baroque in the 16th century and floral themes in the 17th, to art deco and beyond in the 20th.*

# HISTORY AND FOLKLORE

THERE ARE NUMEROUS myths and legends associated with gems. Some tell of cursed stones; others of stones with special powers of healing, or that protect or give good luck to the wearer. Some of the largest known diamonds have legends associated with them that have been told and re-told over centuries, and many now lost are surrounded by tales of intrigue and murder. Some mines are thought to be cursed – probably a rumour spread by the mine-owners to keep unwanted prospectors away. In Burma, for instance, where all gemstones belonged to the monarch, the belief that anyone who took a stone from a mine would be cursed may have been deliberately cultivated to curb losses of a valuable national asset.

**DEATH MASK**
*This Aztec funeral mask adorned with turquoise may have speeded entry to the next world.*

**PERUVIAN GOD**
*This 12th-century ceremonial knife from Peru is made from gold adorned with turquoise. The handle has been formed into the image of a divinity.*

## CRYSTAL GAZING

Since Greek and Roman times, balls of polished rock crystal have been used to see into the future. The difficulty of finding a flawless piece large enough to be polished adds to the mystique. The mystic gazes at the ball, lets the eyes go out of focus, and then interprets the misty "image".

*rock crystal ball supported by Japanese dragons*

**THUMB GUARD**
*This 17th-century ring, mounted with rubies and emeralds, was designed to protect archers' thumbs when releasing arrows.*

**CRYSTAL BALL**

## BIRTHSTONES

Certain gems have traditionally been associated with different months of the year, and are thought lucky or important for people born under their "influence". This probably stems from the ancient belief that gems came from the heavens. Many cultures associate gems with the signs of the zodiac, and others with the months of the year, but the selection varies from country to country, perhaps influenced by availability of gems, local traditions, or fashions. The custom of wearing birthstone jewellery started in 18th-century Poland, and has since spread throughout the world. The most popular selection today is shown right.

**JANUARY** (GARNET)

**FEBRUARY** (AMETHYST)

**MARCH** (AQUAMARINE)

**APRIL** (DIAMOND)

**MAY** (EMERALD)

**JUNE** (PEARL)

**JULY** (RUBY)

**AUGUST** (PERIDOT)

**SEPTEMBER** (SAPPHIRE)

**OCTOBER** (OPAL)

**NOVEMBER** (TOPAZ)

**DECEMBER** (TURQUOISE)

SIGNS OF THE ZODIAC
*This rock crystal is shaped with 12 pentagonal faces, each engraved with one of the signs of the zodiac.*

## CRYSTAL HEALING

Belief in the healing properties of gems has a very long history, as the rituals of medicine men in ancient tribes attest. Crystal healers today believe that each gem has the power to influence the health and well-being of a specific part of the body. The light reflected off stones placed on vital nerve points is thought to be absorbed by the body, supplying it with healing energy.

ROCK CRYSTAL
*Prized for their beauty and clarity, rock crystals are often chosen for use in crystal healing.*

CRYSTAL PENDANT
*Gems worn close to the skin are believed to heal or protect.*

# SYNTHETIC GEMSTONES

SYNTHETIC GEMSTONES are made in laboratories or factories, not in rocks. They have virtually the same chemical composition and crystal structure as natural gemstones, so their optical and physical properties are very similar.

However, they can usually be identified by the differences in their inclusions. Many gems have been synthesized in the laboratory, but only a few are produced commercially – generally for industrial and scientific purposes.

## MAKING A SYNTHETIC

Man has tried to replicate gemstones for thousands of years, but it was not until the late 1800s that any substantial success was achieved. In 1877 French chemist Edmond Frémy grew the first gem-quality crystals of reasonable size (see bottom right), and then around 1900 August Verneuil devised his technique to manufacture ruby. With a few modifications, the Verneuil "flame-fusion" method is still in use today. The powdered ingredients are dropped into a furnace and melt as they fall through a flame hotter than 2,000°C (3,630°F), fusing into liquid drops. These drip on to a pedestal and crystallize. As the pedestal is withdrawn, a long, cylindrical crystal, which is known as a boule, forms.

FLUX-MELT TECHNIQUE
*Pioneered by the French chemist Edmond Frémy, the flux-melt technique is still used to make emeralds. The powdered ingredients are melted and fused in a solvent (flux) in a crucible. The material must be kept at a very high temperature for months, before being left to cool very slowly.*

**FLUX-MELT SYNTHETIC EMERALD**

FLAME-FUSION CORUNDUM
*Synthetic corundum manufactured by flame-fusion grows as a single mass called a "boule". It has the same inner structure as a natural crystal and can be cut to shape.*

*synthetic ruby crystals grown in a crucible* •

*corundum boules tend to split down their length* •

EDMOND FRÉMY
*The first to grow emerald crystals of a reasonable size, French chemist Edmond Frémy went on to grow ruby crystals by melting aluminium oxide and chromium in a crucible.*

• *pedestal on which boule forms*

**CORUNDUM BOULES**

## SHAPES AND COLOURS

Because of the way they are made, synthetic gems may show subtle differences in shape and colour that help to distinguish them from their natural counterparts. For instance, corundum produced by flame-fusion has curved growth lines, rather than straight ones, because the ingredients have not mixed together fully. Some synthetic gems may also suffer from uneven colour distribution. Flame-fusion spinel is manufactured to imitate gems such as ruby, sapphire, aquamarine, blue zircon, tourmaline, peridot, and chrysoberyl.

**SYNTHETIC SPINEL**
*Synthetic spinel (above), coloured red, may make a better imitation gem than flame-fusion ruby (left).*

## DISTINCTIVE INCLUSIONS

Synthetic gems have different inclusions from natural gems, so often the best way to tell them apart is to examine them with a loupe (below) or a microscope. Synthetic inclusions may be typical of a process, or of a synthetic gem species. For instance, in Verneuil rubies, gas bubbles have well-defined outlines; in flux-melt emeralds (right), characteristic "veil" and "feather" patterns form.

**GILSON FLUX-MELT EMERALD**

**GILSON EMERALD INCLUSIONS**
*Synthetic emeralds from the French manufacturer, Gilson, have characteristic veil-like inclusions. The gems are made from poor-quality material by a flux-melt method.*

**LOUPE**
*This hand-held lens is powerful enough to assist in gem identification. With its ten-fold magnification it may be possible to distinguish between natural and synthetic inclusions.*

**GILSON TURQUOISE**

**GILSON LAPIS LAZULI**

**GILSON CORAL**

## GILSON GEMS

Lapis lazuli, turquoise, and coral produced by the French manufacturer, Gilson, are similar to their natural counterparts, but are not true synthetics because their optical and physical properties differ from the natural gems. Gilson lapis lazuli, for example, is more porous and has a lower specific gravity.

# IMITATION AND ENHANCEMENT

IMITATION GEMS have the appearance of their natural counterparts, but their physical properties are different. They are made to deceive. Man-made materials, such as glass and synthetic spinel, have been used to imitate many different gems, but natural stones can also be modified to resemble more valuable gems. It is possible to enhance authentic gemstones by hiding cracks and flaws, or by heat-treating or irradiating to improve their colour.

## GLASS IMITATIONS

Glass has been used for centuries to imitate gemstones. It can be made either transparent or opaque, in almost any colour, and, like many gems, has a vitreous lustre. At first sight, therefore, it may easily be mistaken for the real thing. However, it can usually be detected by its warmer feel, and by the evidence of wear and tear that results from its greater softness. Chipped facets and internal swirls and bubbles are common. In addition, unlike most of the gems it imitates, glass is singly refractive.

GLASS "RUBY"

*glass imitations often contain pronounced inclusions* •

• *glass can be made to imitate almost any transparent gem*

SNOWFLAKE INCLUSION IN GLASS

## OPAL IMITATIONS

Gemmologists call the flashes of colour in opal its "play of colour", or iridescence. It is caused by the interference of light from the minute spheres of silica gel that make up the gem. This structure is imitated to great effect in opals made by the French manufacturer, Gilson, although the difference can be seen in the mosaic-like margins of the patches of colour (see p.135). There are various other opal imitations, including stones made of polystyrene latex, or of different pieces assembled as one. In an opal "doublet" (two pieces) the top is natural precious opal, but the base is common (potch) opal, glass, or chalcedony. A "triplet" (three pieces) has an additional protective dome of rock crystal.

POLYSTYRENE LATEX "OPAL"

GILSON OPAL

### SLOCUM STONES

*The American John Slocum developed imitation opals with a convincing play of colour, but they lack the silky, flat colour patches of genuine opal, and the structure looks crumpled when magnified.*

## GARNET-TOPPED DOUBLET

One of the most common "composite" stones (stones made of more than one piece) is the garnet-topped doublet, or GTD. A thin section of natural garnet is cemented to a coloured glass base, which gives the GTD its apparent colour. The deception is most easily seen at the junction of the two layers, which may be obvious.

red garnet crown •

• green glass base

**GARNET-TOPPED DOUBLET**

GTD JUNCTION
*Changes in colour and lustre are visible where garnet and glass meet.*

## DIAMOND IMITATIONS

Many natural materials have been used to imitate diamond, but zircon is the most convincing. Synthetic imitations are popular, but each has its faults (right). Imitations can usually be detected by testing the heat conductivity of the stone.

• heavy, lacks fire

softer, more fire •

• heavier than diamond

**YTTRIUM ALUMINIUM GARNET (YAG)**

**CUBIC ZIRCONIA**

**STRONTIUM TITANATE**

## HEAT TREATMENT

Heating may enhance or change the colour or clarity of some gems. Techniques range from throwing gems in a fire to "cook", to use of sophisticated equipment. The outcome is certain for some gems (like aquamarine, changing from green to blue), but less so for others.

**BROWN ZIRCON HEATED TO BLUE**

## STAINING

Stains, dyes, or chemicals can alter the appearance of a gem, coating just the surface, or changing the whole specimen. For staining to be effective, a stone must be porous or contain cracks and flaws through which the colour can enter. Porous white howlite, for example, can be stained to imitate turquoise.

**STAINED HOWLITE**

## IRRADIATION

Gems may change colour if exposed to radiation. This may come from radioactive elements within the Earth's crust, or from artificial sources. Natural radiation may take millions of years to have an effect, while artificial irradiation may take only a few hours to change a gem's colour. In some cases a gem will revert to its original colour, or may fade with time. Many changes can be reversed or modified by heat treatment.

**IRRADIATED, HEAT-TREATED TOPAZ**

## OILING

Oils may enhance a gem's colour and disguise fissures and blemishes. It is common to oil emeralds in order to fill their natural cracks and flaws.

**OILED EMERALD**

# COLOUR KEY

WHEN IDENTIFYING a gemstone, a gemmologist will want to hold it, feel it, and examine it from all angles. This is done to assess the appearance of the stone: the lustre, the colour, and any other features. A hand-held loupe (see p.35) may be used to search for scratches and flaws on the surface which may give an indication of hardness, while a search inside the stone may reveal characteristic inclusions. These features may be unique to one gem, but further tests may be necessary to identify synthetic or imitation stones. From this initial examination, however, the gemmologist should know which tests to perform.

## HOW THE COLOUR KEY WORKS

This key puts all gems into one of seven colour categories, though colour varieties within some species may appear (or be listed, if not pictured in the book itself) in more than one. Each colour category is divided into three sections: gems that are always that colour, gems usually that colour, and gems sometimes that colour.

*category heading*

• *representative specimen*

*gem name* •

*key identification features* •

**RUBY** *94*
*Distinctive red colour; hard*

• *page number of main entry*

**RUBY**

**ALMANDINE GARNET**

**RED GLASS**

SPECTROSCOPE
*Many gems appear the same colour, but can be distinguished when viewed with a spectroscope (above). This reveals an absorption spectrum (left) that is unique to each gemstone (see p.21).*

## COLOURLESS GEMSTONES

### ALWAYS COLOURLESS

**HAMBERGITE** *115*
*Perfect cleavage, large birefringence*

**PHENAKITE** *98*
*Silvery look if well cut*

**ALBITE** *130*
*Vitreous to pearly lustre*

**GOSHENITE** *77*
*Spiky inclusions common*

**BERYLLONITE** *118*
*Lacks fire, soft, brittle*

ROCK CRYSTAL *81*
*Vitreous lustre,
transparent*

PETALITE *129*
*Vitreous lustre,
transparent*

DATOLITE *129*
*Tinge of yellow,
green, or white*

ACHROITE *102*
*Extremely
rare*

**USUALLY COLOURLESS**

SCHEELITE *70*
*Quite soft, good
fire, uncommon*

CELESTINE *105*
*Soft, cut for
collectors only*

DIAMOND *54*
*Adamantine
lustre, good fire*

DANBURITE *110*
*Yellow/pink tinge,
bright, lacks fire*

CERUSSITE *105*
*Adamantine lustre,
high density, soft*

**SOMETIMES COLOURLESS**

DOLOMITE *99*
*Soft, vitreous
to pearly lustre*

EUCLASE *129*
*Rare, black
mineral inclusions*

MOONSTONE *123*
*Opalescence, blue
or white sheen*

COLOURLESS
ORTHOCLASE *122*
*Three good cleavages*

SCAPOLITE *71*
*Rare, vitreous
lustre*

**OTHER GEMS**
ENSTATITE *111*
GROSSULAR *61*
TOPAZ *106*

FLUORITE *66*
*Soft, lacks fire,
hematite inclusions*

ZIRCON *72*
*Adamantine
lustre, good fire*

SAPPHIRE *96*
*Rare, high density,
extremely hard*

APATITE *79*
*Fairly soft*

## RED OR PINK

### ALWAYS RED OR PINK

**ROSE QUARTZ** *83*
*Cloudy, distinctive
pinkish colour*

**KUNZITE** *120*
*Strongly pleochroic,
good cleavage*

**MORGANITE** *78*
*Distinctive
colour; hard*

**THULITE** *116*
*Distinctive colour
mix, massive*

**PINK GROSSULAR** *60*
*Distinctive colour;
fine-grained, opaque*

**TUGTUPITE** *74*
*Opaque, may be
mottled, massive*

**RHODOCHROSITE** *100*
*Fine-grained, banded;
also clear faceted stones*

**RHODONITE** *132*
*Black veins in
massive material*

**RED BERYL** *78*
*Extremely rare,
seldom cut*

**RUBY** *94*
*Distinctive red
colour, hard*

### USUALLY RED OR PINK

**ALMANDINE** *59*
*Distinctive colour,
high lustre*

**PYROPE** *58*
*Distinctive colour,
inclusions rare*

**RUBELLITE** *101*
*Pleochroic, cat's-
eye cabochons*

**TAAFFEITE** *80*
*Extremely rare,
fairly hard*

**SPESSARTINE** *58*
*Lace-like inclusions,
rare at gem-quality*

### SOMETIMES RED OR PINK

**JADEITE** *124*
*Dimpled surface
when polished*

**TOPAZ** *106*
*Distinctive colour,
hard, high density*

**WATERMELON
TOURMALINE** *103*
*Distinctive colours*

**SAPPHIRE** *97*
*High density,
hard, pleochroic*

**CORAL** *142*
*Grain on surface,*
*soft, may fade*

**SPINEL** *64*
*Hard, singly*
*refractive*

**JASPER** *92*
*Distinctive*
*colour, opaque*

**OTHER GEMS**
ZIRCON *73*
RUTILE *71*
SMITHSONITE *99*
SCAPOLITE *71*
GARNET-TOPPED
DOUBLET *61*

## WHITE OR SILVER

### ALWAYS WHITE OR SILVER

**MILKY QUARTZ** *85*
*Distinctive milky*
*white colour*

**PLATINUM** *52*
*Metallic lustre, high*
*density, opaque*

**SILVER** *50*
*Metallic lustre,*
*soft, opaque*

**HOWLITE** *128*
*Very soft,*
*chalky, opaque*

**IVORY** *146*
*Soft, growth*
*lines on surface*

**MEERSCHAUM** *119*
*Chalky, opaque,*
*fine-grained, soft*

**GYPSUM** *128*
*Silky to vitreous*
*lustre, soft*

### USUALLY WHITE OR SILVER

**PEARL** *138*
*Pearly lustre,*
*very soft*

**SHELL** *144*
*Iridescent,*
*very soft*

### SOMETIMES WHITE OR SILVER

**CALCITE** *98*
*Soft, large*
*birefringence*

**SERPENTINE** *127*
*Vitreous to greasy*
*lustre, translucent*

**NEPHRITE** *125*
*Tough interlocking*
*structure*

**OTHER GEMS**
AGATE *88*
CORAL *142*
OPAL *134*
MOONSTONE *123*

# YELLOW TO BROWN GEMSTONES

## ALWAYS YELLOW–BROWN

**ANGLESITE** *114*
*High density,
fragile, good fire*

**CITRINE** *83*
*Distinctive
colour*

**BRAZILIANITE** *118*
*Fragile, brittle,
fairly soft, rare*

**SINHALITE** *114*
*Pleochroic, large
birefringence*

**HELIODOR** *77*
*Pleochroic, hard,
pastel shades*

**GOLD** *48*
*Distinctive
colour, soft*

**PADPARADSCHA** *95*
*Distinctive orange-
pink colour, hard*

**CARNELIAN** *93*
*Translucent,
reddish brown*

**FIRE OPAL** *134*
*Low density,
transparent*

**SARDONYX** *90*
*Distinctive white
bands*

**HESSONITE** *60*
*Granular
inclusions*

**SUNSTONE** *130*
*Bright metallic
inclusions*

**HYPERSTHENE** *112*
*Reddish iridescence,
fairly soft*

**DRAVITE** *102*
*Pleochroic, showing two
shades of body colour*

**CASSITERITE** *70*
*High density,
good fire*

**TORTOISESHELL** *144*
*Distinctive mottling
on surface*

**SMOKY QUARTZ** *84*
*Distinctive greyish
brown colour*

**EPIDOTE** *121*
*Strongly pleochroic,
fragile, rarely cut*

**OTHER GEMS**
TOPAZOLITE *107*
PYRITE *63*

COLOUR KEY • 43

## USUALLY YELLOW-BROWN

**AMBLYGONITE** *132*
*Vitreous to pearly lustre*

**YELLOW ORTHOCLASE** *122*
*Fragile, cat's-eyes*

**VESUVIANITE** *74*
*Pleochroic, vitreous to adamantine lustre*

**SPHALERITE** *63*
*Good fire, metallic to vitreous lustre*

**TITANITE** *121*
*Very good fire, pleochroic*

**AMBER** *148*
*Very soft, resinous lustre*

**AVENTURINE QUARTZ** *85*
*Platy inclusions*

**AXINITE** *133*
*Pleochroic, easily chipped*

**ENSTATITE** *111*
*Fragile, distinctive absorption spectrum*

**STAUROLITE** *117*
*Opaque, twinned crystals cross-shaped*

## SOMETIMES YELLOW-BROWN

**RUTILE** *71*
*Good fire, needle-like inclusions*

**PREHNITE** *115*
*Usually cloudy and translucent*

**SCHEELITE** *70*
*Fairly soft, good fire*

**CHATOYANT QUARTZ** *86*
*Fibrous structure*

**MOSS AGATE** *89*
*Translucent, moss-like pattern*

**ARAGONITE** *104*
*Very soft, micro-crystalline*

**SPESSARTINE** *58*
*Hard, lace-like inclusions*

**BARYTE** *104*
*High density, very soft*

**CHRYSOBERYL** *108*
*Hard, strongly pleochroic*

**OTHER GEMS**
DIAMOND *54*
DEMANTOID *62*
FLUORITE *66*
ZIRCON *72*
APATITE *79*
SAPPHIRE *96*
TOURMALINE *101*
TOPAZ *106*
KORNERUPINE *113*

## GREEN GEMSTONES

### ALWAYS GREEN

**CHRYSOCOLLA** *126*
*Distinctive colour,
opaque, very soft*

**EMERALD** *75*
*Distinctive colour,
seldom flawless*

**PERIDOT** *113*
*Distinctive oily
green colour*

**HIDDENITE** *120*
*Distinctive
colour; pleochroic*

**DIOPTASE** *99*
*Distinctive colour,
large birefringence*

**BLOODSTONE** *93*
*Opaque, red
spots*

**UVAROVITE** *59*
*Distinctive colour,
crystals fragile*

**PRASE** *92*
*Translucent, dark
green colour*

**MALACHITE** *126*
*Characteristic bands
of colour, soft*

**MOLDAVITE** *137*
*Glassy, inclusions of
bubbles and swirls*

**ALEXANDRITE** *108*
*Colour changes,
pleochroic, high density*

**ANDALUSITE** *110*
*Very strong
pleochroism*

### USUALLY GREEN

**SERPENTINE** *127*
*Vitreous to greasy
lustre, fairly soft*

**JADEITE** *124*
*Fine-grained,
may be dimpled*

**DIOPSIDE** *119*
*Large
birefringence*

**DEMANTOID** *62*
*Asbestos inclusions,
adamantine lustre*

**OTHER GEMS**
PREHNITE *115*

**AVENTURINE QUARTZ** *85*
*Platy inclusions,
vitreous lustre*

**NEPHRITE** *125*
*Tough interlocking structure,
greasy to pearly lustre*

## SOMETIMES GREEN

**MICROCLINE** *123*
*Distinctive blue-
green colour*

**AGATE** *88*
*Translucent,
distinct banding*

**WATERMELON
TOURMALINE** *103*
*Bicoloured*

**DIAMOND** *56*
*Hardest natural
substance, good fire*

**SAPPHIRE** *96*
*High density,
hard, pleochroic*

**APATITE** *79*
*Distinctive
absorption spectrum*

**ZIRCON** *72*
*Good fire, adaman-
tine to resinous lustre*

**GROSSULAR
GARNET** *61*
*Vitreous lustre*

**GARNET-TOPPED
DOUBLET** *61*
*Two parts joined*

**ENSTATITE** *111*
*Distinctive
absorption spectrum*

**OTHER GEMS**
FLUORITE *66*
KYANITE *133*
TOURMALINE *103*
SMITHSONITE *99*
EUCLASE *129*

**KORNERUPINE** *113*
*Strongly pleochroic,
rare as gem-quality*

**SPHALERITE** *63*
*Very soft, good
fire, high density*

## BLUE OR VIOLET GEMSTONES

### ALWAYS BLUE OR VIOLET

**AQUAMARINE** *76*
*Tubular inclusions,*
*pleochroic*

**LAZULITE** *128*
*Often*
*mottled*

**HAUYNE** *68*
*Small stones,*
*rarely cut*

**TURQUOISE** *131*
*Distinctive*
*colour, fragile*

**INDICOLITE** *101*
*Strongly*
*pleochroic*

**AZURITE** *126*
*Distinctive colour,*
*fragile, soft*

**LAPIS LAZULI** *69*
*Distinctive blue,*
*pyrite inclusions*

**SODALITE** *68*
*Distinctive*
*blue colour*

**ZOISITE** *116*
*Strongly*
*pleochroic*

**AMETHYST** *82*
*Tiger-stripe*
*inclusions*

### USUALLY BLUE OR VIOLET

**SILLIMANITE** *111*
*Distinctly pleochroic,*
*good cleavage*

**DUMORTIERITE** *117*
*Usually massive,*
*distinctive colour*

**BENITOITE** *80*
*Good fire,*
*birefringence*

**IOLITE** *112*
*Strongly*
*pleochroic*

**KYANITE** *133*
*Pleochroic,*
*brittle, flaky*

### SOMETIMES BLUE OR VIOLET

**FLUORITE** *66*
*Lacks fire, soft,*
*good cleavages*

**TOPAZ** *106*
*Pleochroic, hard,*
*tear-like inclusions*

**ZIRCON** *72*
*Good fire, adaman-*
*tine to resinous lustre*

**SMITHSONITE** *99*
*Distinctive*
*blue colour*

**SAPPHIRE** *95*
*High density,*
*hard, pleochroic*

**SCAPOLITE** *71*
*Cat's-eyes, fibrous inclusions*

**SPINEL** *64*
*Hard, singly refractive*

**AXINITE** *133*
*Pleochroic, brittle*

**OTHER GEMS**
APATITE *79*
AGATE (STAINED) *88*
HOWLITE (STAINED) *128*
DIAMOND *54*
EUCLASE *129*
CHRYSOBERYL *108*
GARNET-TOPPED DOUBLET *61*

## BLACK GEMSTONES

### ALWAYS BLACK

**HEMATITE** *100*
*Metallic lustre, opaque, iridescent*

**SCHORL** *103*
*Opaque, vitreous lustre*

**JET** *140*
*Very soft, coal-like smell when warm*

### USUALLY BLACK

**OBSIDIAN** *136*
*Glassy, fairly hard, bubble-like inclusions*

### SOMETIMES BLACK

**MELANITE** *62*
*Adamantine to vitreous lustre*

**DIAMOND** *54*
*Adamantine lustre, hard*

**TEKTITE** *137*
*Glassy, cracks on surface*

**CORAL** *142*
*Sensitive to heat, soft*

## IRIDESCENT GEMSTONES

**OPAL** *134*
*Iridescent colours, may dry and crack*

**FIRE AGATE** *87*
*Iridescence resembles oily rings of colour*

**LABRADORITE** *130*
*Iridescence on dark body colour*

**MOTHER-OF-PEARL** *145*
*Blue and purple iridescence on surface*

| Crystal structure Cubic | Composition Gold | | Hardness 2½ |
|---|---|---|---|

# GOLD

The colour of gold depends upon the amount and type of impurities it contains. Native gold is typically golden yellow, but in order to vary its colour and increase its hardness for use in jewellery, gold may be alloyed to other metals. Silver, platinum, nickel, or zinc may be added to give a pale or white gold. Copper is added for red or pink gold; iron for a tinge of blue. Gold purity is defined by the proportion of pure gold metal present, and this is expressed as its carat (ct) value. The purity of gold used in jewellery varies from 9 carat (37½ per cent or more pure gold), through 14, 18, and 22 carat, to 24 carat, which is pure gold. In many countries, gold is "hallmarked" to indicate its degree of purity.

smooth, waterworn
• surface

GOLD NUGGET
• metallic lustre

• **OCCURRENCE** Gold is found in igneous rocks and in associated quartz veins, often in small quantities invisible to the naked eye. It is also concentrated in secondary "placer" deposits – as nuggets or grains in river sands and gravels. Gold may still be extracted from placer deposits by the traditional panning method, but modern commercial mining involves large earth-moving machinery and concentrated acids for processing the ore. The main gold-bearing rocks occur in Africa, California and Alaska (USA), Canada, the former USSR, South America, and Australia.

octahedral crystals of gold in a skeletal framework •

• **REMARK** Gold has been used for coins, decoration, and jewellery for thousands of years. It is attractive, easily worked, and wears well.

CRYSTALLIZED GOLD NUGGET

typically rounded and flattened grains •

grains collected from placer deposits by • panning

white • quartz

gold usually • occurs as fine grains, not groups of crystals like these

GOLD GRAINS

GOLD IN QUARTZ MATRIX

| SG 19.30 | RI None | DR None | Lustre Metallic |
|---|---|---|---|

- *crystalline nugget*

**TIE-PIN**
This unusual piece of jewellery features a gold nugget set into a gold tie-pin.

**GOLD, DIAMONDS, AND PEARLS**
This gold neckpiece is set with pink pearls and clusters of diamonds. Gold is a popular setting for precious stones as it is both easy to fashion and hard-wearing, being resistant to acids and tarnishing.

*groups of*
• *diamonds*

*natural*
• *pearl*

**GOLD BANGLE**
This flexible bracelet is made from 18-carat red and yellow gold.

**GOLD MOULD**
This ivy leaf motif set was made by casting 18-carat gold in a wax mould.

• *hallmark*

**GOLD BANGLE**
The hallmark that shows the purity of worked gold is just visible on this delicate bangle. In this case, it indicates the gold is 18 carat.

*softness of gold* •
*accommodates*
*intricate working*

**GOLD RING**
Gold is a popular and resilient material for finger rings. Here it is the setting for a green demantoid garnet.

*square-cut* •
*demantoid garnet*

| Crystal structure Cubic | Composition Silver | | Hardness 2½ |
|---|---|---|---|

# SILVER

Silver usually occurs in massive form as nuggets or grains, although it may also be found in wiry, dendritic (tree-like) aggregates. When newly mined or recently polished, it has a characteristic bright, silver-white colour and metallic lustre. However, on exposure to oxygen in the air a black layer of silver oxide readily forms, tarnishing the surface. Because of this, and the fact that it is too soft to be used in most jewellery in its pure form, silver is often alloyed with other metals, or given a covering layer of gold. Electrum, an alloy of gold and silver in use since the time of the Ancient Greeks, contains 20–25 per cent silver. Sterling silver contains 92½ per cent or more pure silver (and usually some copper), and Britannia silver has a silver content of 95 per cent or more. Both alloys are used as standards to define silver content.
• OCCURRENCE Most silver is a by-product of lead mining, and is often associated with copper. The main silver mining areas of the world are South America, the USA, Australia, and the former USSR. The greatest single producer of silver is probably Mexico, where silver has been mined from about AD1500 to the present day. The finest native silver, which occurs naturally in the shape of twisted wire, is from Kongsberg, Norway.

*surface tarnished • by silver oxide*

*natural, branch- • like habit*

**DENDRITIC SILVER CRYSTALS**

*• polished silver*

*patches of copper •*

**POLISHED SLICE OF SILVER AND COPPER ORE**

*maker's • mark*

*crystals have wire-like habit •*

*dendritic silver from Kongsberg is renowned for • its quality*

**SILVER WINE CUP**
This part-gilt silver cup was fashioned in 1493, when silver was valued as highly as gold.

**NATIVE SILVER FROM KONGSBERG, NORWAY**

| SG 10.50 | RI None | DR None | Lustre Metallic |
|---|---|---|---|

• red gold

• yellow gold

**TOWER BROOCHES**
These modern silver brooches, made by British silversmith, V. Ambery-Smith, have additional decoration in red and yellow gold.

• silver

*18-carat gold thread* •

• *highly polished silver*

**SILVER BRACELET**
This sterling silver bracelet also features 18-carat gold thread.

**SILVER DISH**
Fashioned in 1973, this dish features a leaf motif border made from oxidized silver.

*oxidation alters colour* • *of silver*

*ornate carving* •

**WATCH CASE**
Because of its softness, silver is extremely popular for fine metalwork, as seen in this 18th century watch.

*silver lends a simple elegance to modern designs* •

**MODERN USES**
Silver is prized for ornamental items, such as these key rings. Today it is also used in the electronics and photographic industries.

| Crystal structure Cubic | Composition Platinum | Hardness 4 |
|---|---|---|

# PLATINUM

Platinum has been used for thousands of years, but it was not recognized as a chemical element until 1735. Of the three precious metals – gold, silver, and platinum – it is the rarest and the most valuable. Chemically inert and resistant to corrosion, platinum does not tarnish when exposed to the atmosphere, unlike silver. It is silvery grey, grey-white, or white in colour, opaque, and has a metallic lustre. It is slightly more dense than pure gold and about twice as dense as silver. Early jewellers had difficulty achieving the 1,773°C (3,223°F) needed to melt platinum: it was not until the 1920s that the technology was developed sufficiently to work this precious metal.

• OCCURRENCE Platinum forms in igneous rocks, usually as ores in which the grains of platinum are often too minute to be seen with the naked eye. It may also occur in secondary "placer" deposits in river sands and gravels, and glacial deposits – usually as grains, more rarely as nuggets. The main occurrences of platinum have been in South Africa, Canada (Sudbury), the USA (Alaska), Russia (the River Perm and other rivers running down from the Urals), Australia, Colombia, and Peru.

• REMARK Although nuggets had been set in rings before 1920, most platinum jewellery dates from after this time. Soft and easy to work, platinum is often fashioned into quite intricate designs.

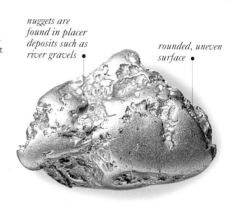

*nuggets are found in placer deposits such as river gravels*

*rounded, uneven surface*

PLATINUM NUGGET

*isolated crystals are rare in nature*

*distinct cubic structure*

ISOLATED CRYSTALS

*silvery colour*

*grains are found in secondary deposits, rarely in the host rock*

*opaque, with metallic lustre*

*cavities denote position of original matrix*

PLATINUM GRAINS

CRYSTALLIZED PLATINUM

| SG 21.40 | RI None | DR None | Lustre Metallic |
|---|---|---|---|

**RING AND EARRING SUITE**
This modern suite is set with square-cut precious stones in all the colours of the rainbow.

**FILIGREE NECKLACE**
Like gold and silver, platinum is quite a soft material, making it ideal for the sort of intricate working seen in this necklace. Unlike silver, platinum does not tarnish when exposed to the atmosphere.

• *platinum setting*

• *platinum filigree*

**MODERN BROOCH**
Platinum is a popular and stylish material for modern jewellery.

*diamond-set detail at back of necklace* •

*two hoops provide framework for design* •

**NECKLACE WITH DIAMONDS**
Platinum is a perfect, if very expensive, setting for cut diamonds, as the colours complement each other well.

*pendeloque-cut aquamarine* •

*diamonds* •

*inlaid diamonds* •

*pendeloque-cut aquamarine* •

**AQUAMARINE RING**
Platinum provides a cool setting for this ice-blue pendeloque-cut aquamarine and its twenty diamonds.

| Crystal structure Cubic | Composition Carbon | Hardness 10 |
|---|---|---|

# DIAMOND

Diamond is the hardest mineral on Earth, and this, combined with its exceptional lustre and brilliant fire, has made it the most highly prized of all gems. Pure, colourless diamond is the most popular, but other varieties – from yellow and brown to green, blue, pink, red, grey, and black – are also found, depending on the impurities present. Because of the uniform arrangement of their constituent carbon atoms, diamond crystals are well-formed – usually octahedral with rounded edges and slightly convex faces. Their perfect cleavage facilitates the early stages of fashioning (see p.26), but they can only be polished by other diamonds.

• OCCURRENCE Diamond forms at high temperatures and pressures 80km (50 miles) or more underground. When India and later Brazil were the main producers, most diamond came from secondary sources, such as river gravels. However, since the discovery of diamond in kimberlite rock in South Africa (around 1870), its extraction has involved processing vast quantities of rock. Australia is the main producer today; other localities include Ghana, Sierra Leone, Zaire, Botswana, Namibia, the former USSR, the USA, and Brazil.

• REMARK Diamonds are graded by colour, cut, clarity, and carat (weight) – the four c's.

• coloured diamonds, such as this yellowish green variety, are known as "fancy"

BRILLIANT-CUT

most diamonds • are faceted as a brilliant-cut, which brings out their natural fire

BRILLIANT-CUT

• brilliant-cut reflects as much light as possible out through front of stone

pale pink stone •

BRILLIANT-CUT

subtle grey-green colour •

• minimum light leakage through back facets

BRILLIANT-CUT

pink-red • variety

diamonds may be transparent • to opaque

green and black inclusions •

typical convex surfaces •

adamantine lustre •

rounded edges •

FIVE UNPOLISHED DIAMOND CRYSTALS

| SG 3.52 | RI 2.42 | DR None | Lustre Adamantine |
|---|---|---|---|

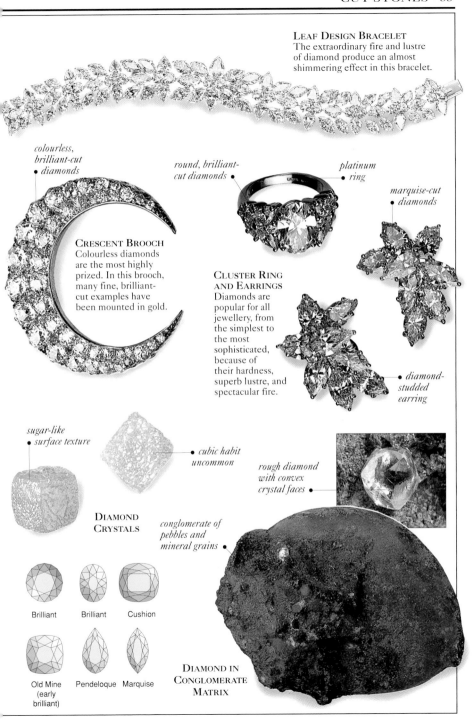

**LEAF DESIGN BRACELET**
The extraordinary fire and lustre of diamond produce an almost shimmering effect in this bracelet.

*colourless, brilliant-cut • diamonds*

*round, brilliant-cut diamonds •*

*platinum • ring*

*marquise-cut • diamonds*

**CRESCENT BROOCH**
Colourless diamonds are the most highly prized. In this brooch, many fine, brilliant-cut examples have been mounted in gold.

**CLUSTER RING AND EARRINGS**
Diamonds are popular for all jewellery, from the simplest to the most sophisticated, because of their hardness, superb lustre, and spectacular fire.

*• diamond-studded earring*

*sugar-like • surface texture*

*• cubic habit uncommon*

*rough diamond with convex crystal faces •*

**DIAMOND CRYSTALS**

*conglomerate of pebbles and mineral grains •*

Brilliant

Brilliant

Cushion

Old Mine (early brilliant)

Pendeloque

Marquise

**DIAMOND IN CONGLOMERATE MATRIX**

| Crystal structure Cubic | Composition Carbon | | Hardness 10 |
|---|---|---|---|

• *different colour varieties are caused by minute traces of other minerals*

• *unusual, semi-translucent, milky white stone*

*opaque, black "bort" variety derives colour from graphite*
• *inclusions*

Inclusions in this diamond cause asterism in the form of a double six-rayed star.

**BRILLIANT-CUT**

*pinkish brown colour* •

*colourless stone marred by black, carbon-filled*
• *inclusions*

**BRILLIANT-CUT BORT DIAMOND**

*dodecahedral (12-sided)*
• *habit*

**BRILLIANT-CUT**

**BRILLIANT-CUT**

*dark green colour due to exposure to radioactive radium* •

*colourless diamond*
• *crystal*

*volcanic, diamond-bearing kimberlite rock, first identified in Kimberley,*
• *South Africa*

**DIAMOND CRYSTAL**

*characteristic three-sided face, known*
• *as a trigon*

**FANCY DIAMOND CRYSTAL**

**DIAMOND IN KIMBERLITE**

| SG 3.52 | RI 2.42 | DR None | Lustre Adamantine |
|---|---|---|---|

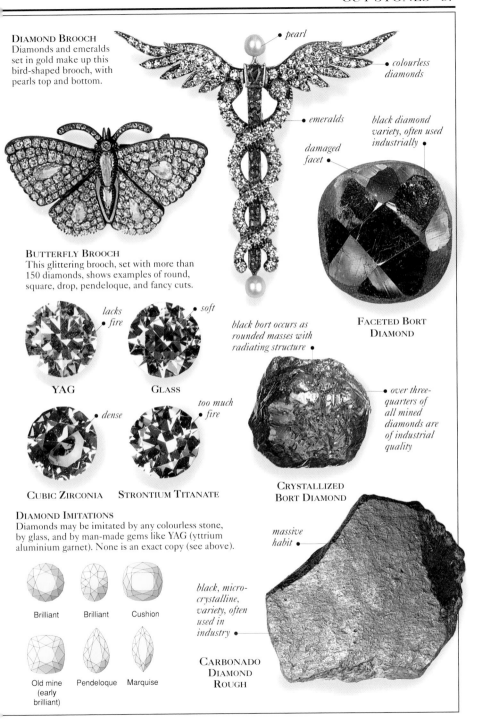

**DIAMOND BROOCH**
Diamonds and emeralds set in gold make up this bird-shaped brooch, with pearls top and bottom.

• pearl

• colourless diamonds

• emeralds

black diamond variety, often used industrially •

damaged facet •

**BUTTERFLY BROOCH**
This glittering brooch, set with more than 150 diamonds, shows examples of round, square, drop, pendeloque, and fancy cuts.

lacks • fire

• soft

black bort occurs as rounded masses with radiating structure •

**FACETED BORT DIAMOND**

**YAG**

**GLASS**

too much • fire

• dense

• over three-quarters of all mined diamonds are of industrial quality

**CUBIC ZIRCONIA**    **STRONTIUM TITANATE**

**CRYSTALLIZED BORT DIAMOND**

**DIAMOND IMITATIONS**
Diamonds may be imitated by any colourless stone, by glass, and by man-made gems like YAG (yttrium aluminium garnet). None is an exact copy (see above).

massive habit •

Brilliant    Brilliant    Cushion

black, micro-crystalline, variety, often used in industry •

Old mine    Pendeloque    Marquise
(early brilliant)

**CARBONADO DIAMOND ROUGH**

| Crystal structure Cubic | Composition Magnesium aluminium silicate | Hardness 7¼ |
| --- | --- | --- |

# PYROPE (GARNET)

The blood-red colour of pyrope is due to its iron and chromium content. It rarely has inclusions, but when present they are rounded crystals or have irregular outlines. As with all garnets, pyrope has no cleavage, and fracture is subconchoidal to uneven.
• OCCURRENCE Pyrope is found in volcanic rock and alluvial deposits, and may, along with certain other minerals, indicate the presence of diamond-bearing rocks. Localities include Arizona (USA), South Africa, Argentina, Australia, Brazil, Burma, Scotland, Switzerland, and Tanzania.
• REMARK Pyrope comes from the Greek *pyropos*, meaning fiery. Swiss and South African pyropes are lighter red than stones from Bohemia, where pyrope jewellery has been made for over 500 years.

*brilliant-cut crown*

*vitreous lustre*

OVAL BRILLIANT

BOHEMIAN EARRINGS
Perfectly transparent, clear, uniformly coloured crystals like these were popular for jewellery in the 18th and 19th centuries.

*hornblende schist matrix*

*pyrope crystals*

*fiery red Bohemian pyrope*

PYROPE CRYSTALS IN MATRIX

Brilliant   Mixed

| SG 3.80 | RI 1.72–1.76 | DR None | Lustre Vitreous |
| --- | --- | --- | --- |

| Crystal structure Cubic | Composition Manganese aluminium silicate | Hardness 7 |
| --- | --- | --- |

# SPESSARTINE (GARNET)

Gem-quality spessartine is uncommon. It is bright orange when pure, but an increase in the iron content makes the stone darker orange to red. Inclusions are lace- or feather-like.
• OCCURRENCE Spessartine occurs in granitic pegmatites and alluvial deposits. It is found in Sri Lanka, Madagascar, Brazil, Sweden, Australia, Burma, and the USA; also Germany and Italy, but crystals there are too small to facet.
• REMARK Spessartine is named after the Spessart district of Bavaria, Germany. It can be confused with hessonite garnet or yellow topaz, but on close examination of inclusions it is distinguishable.

*liquid inclusions*

*vitreous lustre*

OCTAGONAL STEP-CUT

*lace-like inclusions*

*flat crystal face*

CABOCHON

SPESSARTINE CRYSTAL

Brilliant   Step   Cabochon

| SG 4.16 | RI 1.79–1.81 | DR None | Lustre Vitreous |
| --- | --- | --- | --- |

| Crystal structure Cubic | Composition Iron aluminium silicate | Hardness 7½ |
|---|---|---|

# ALMANDINE (GARNET)

Almandine is generally darker red than pyrope and may appear black, although pinkish red specimens are found. It is usually opaque or subtranslucent, but the rare transparent stones have high lustre. Although dense, almandine is brittle and facet edges chip. Many stones show characteristic inclusions, and four-rayed stars may be seen when the stones are cut *en cabochon*. The darker almandines are frequently cut as cabochons or used as abrasives in garnet paper. The underside of dark almandine is often hollowed out to let more light filter through the stone.

• OCCURRENCE Almandine is found in metamorphic rocks, such as garnet mica schist, and less frequently in granitic pegmatites. It has a worldwide occurrence.

• REMARK Slices of garnet have been used in windows in churches and temples, and legend has it that Noah suspended garnet in the ark in order to disperse light. Garnet was once said to cure melancholy and to warm the heart.

• *brilliant-cut enhances fiery red colour*

ROUND BRILLIANT-CUT

Needle-like crystals of rutile or hornblende are typical inclusions in almandine.

*hollow back allows • in more light*

*black mineral inclusions •*

CABOCHON

DROP EARRINGS
The pale pinkish red almandine garnets of this 18th-century pair of earrings have been faceted in the rose-cut, and set in gold.

*rounded almandine crystals •*

*granulite matrix*

*• cut shows triangular faces*

ALMANDINE
CRYSTALS IN MATRIX

Cabochon         Mixed

| SG 4.00 | RI 1.76–1.83 | DR None | Lustre Vitreous |
|---|---|---|---|

| Crystal structure Cubic | Composition Calcium chromium silicate | Hardness 7½ |
|---|---|---|

# UVAROVITE (GARNET)

The attractive, bright green colour of uvarovite is due to the presence of chromium. The crystals are very fragile, with subconchoidal to uneven fracture.

• OCCURRENCE Uvarovite occurs in serpentine rocks. The best clear crystals are found in the Urals in Russia, lining cavities or rock fissures. Other sources are Finland, Turkey, and Italy.

*striations on crystal • face*

*uvarovite crystal •*

*skarn • matrix*

Brilliant

UVAROVITE CRYSTAL

UVAROVITE CRYSTALS
IN MATRIX

| SG 3.77 | RI 1.86–1.87 | DR None | Lustre Vitreous |
|---|---|---|---|

| Crystal structure Cubic | Composition Calcium aluminium silicate | Hardness 7¼ |
|---|---|---|

# HESSONITE (GROSSULAR GARNET)

cinnamon-coloured stone

OVAL MIXED-CUT

Hessonite garnet has swirls of inclusions, giving it a treacly appearance.

Grossular garnets occur in a very wide range of colours, from colourless right through to black, but derive their name from the first specimen found, a distinctive gooseberry-green colour (see opposite). The orange-brown colour of hessonite grossular garnet is due to manganese and iron inclusions.
• OCCURRENCE The best hessonite garnets are found in Sri Lanka in metamorphic rocks, or gem gravels and sands. In Madagascar hessonite is often referred to as cinnamon stone. Other local-ities include Brazil, Canada, and Siberia (Russia), as well as Maine, California, and New Hampshire in the USA.
• REMARK Both the Ancient Greeks and Romans made cameos, intaglios, and cabochons from hessonite, and faceted stones for jewellery.

granular inclusions •

• colour due to manganese and iron

bright orange-brown hessonite crystals

hessonite has no cleavage •

OVAL MIXED-CUT

twinned crystals •

Brilliant        Mixed

ROUND MIXED-CUT

HESSONITE CRYSTALS ON MATRIX

| SG 3.65 | RI 1.73–1.75 | DR None | Lustre Vitreous to resinous |
|---|---|---|---|

| Crystal structure Cubic | Composition Calcium aluminium silicate | Hardness 7 |
|---|---|---|

# PINK GROSSULAR (GARNET)

Pure grossular garnet is colourless, but impurities incorporated during its formation cause a wide range of colours. This pink variety results from the presence of iron.
• OCCURRENCE Pink grossular is found in Mexico, usually as a massive form in metamorphic rocks. Crystals are rare. It also occurs in South Africa.
• REMARK Pinkish grossular from Mexico may be known as rosolite.

limestone matrix •

pink grossular crystals •

CRYSTALS IN MATRIX

• pink and green banded material may be called Transvaal jade

Polished

GROSSULAR GARNET POLISHED SLAB

| SG 3.49 | RI 1.69–1.73 | DR None | Lustre Vitreous |
|---|---|---|---|

| Crystal structure Cubic | Composition Calcium aluminium silicate | Hardness 7 |
|---|---|---|

# GREEN GROSSULAR (GARNET)

*chromium and vanadium create • rich green colour*

There are two varieties of green grossular: one is found as transparent crystals, the other is massive. Massive green grossular from South Africa is called Transvaal jade, after its main locality and because it resembles jade. It may contain black specks of the mineral magnetite. Since the 1960s a transparent, green grossular garnet, named tsavorite, has been mined in Kenya. Massive green grossular is used as a decorative stone; tsavorite is faceted as a gem.

BRILLIANT-CUT

*distinctive gooseberry • colour*

**BEAD NECKLACE** Polished massive green grossular beads have a speckly appearance due to magnetite inclusions.

• **OCCURRENCE** Found in Canada, Sri Lanka, Pakistan, the former USSR, Tanzania, South Africa, and the USA. Kenya is the main source for tsavorite.
• **REMARK** The name "grossular" is derived from the botanical name of the gooseberry, *R. grossularia*. Massive grossular garnet of a gooseberry-green colour was first discovered in the former USSR. Since then it has also been found in Hungary and Italy.

*groups of green grossular crystals •*

Brilliant    Bead    Polished

**MASSIVE POLISHED SLAB**

**GREEN GROSSULAR CRYSTALS IN MATRIX**

| SG 3.49 | RI 1.69–1.73 | DR None | Lustre Vitreous |
|---|---|---|---|

| Crystal structure Variable | Composition Variable | Hardness Variable |
|---|---|---|

# GARNET-TOPPED DOUBLET

*red almandine garnet cemented to • green glass base*

A doublet is a stone made of two separate pieces cemented together to create the appearance of a precious stone. Glass topped by red almandine garnet is the most common form, with green glass used to imitate emerald, blue to imitate sapphire. Once joined, the stone is faceted and polished.

*lustre and colour change at junction of stones •*

• **REMARK** These stones were very popular in Britain and the rest of Europe in the Victorian era.

Brilliant    Brilliant

**CUSHION-CUT DOUBLET**

**ALMANDINE GARNET ON GLASS BASE**

| SG Variable | RI Variable | DR None | Lustre Variable |
|---|---|---|---|

| Crystal structure Cubic | Composition Calcium iron silicate | Hardness 6½ |
|---|---|---|

# ANDRADITE GARNET

Garnets containing titanium and manganese are grouped as andradite garnet. The most valuable is demantoid, whose emerald-green colour is due to the presence of chromium. It has a higher dispersion than diamond and can be recognized by the characteristic "horsetails", which are fine, hair-like inclusions of asbestos. Topazolite, the yellow variety of andradite garnet, varies from pale to dark yellow. Only small crystals are found. Melanite is a generally black form, but can also be dark red.

• **OCCURRENCE** The best demantoid is found in the Urals in Russia, and is associated with gold-bearing sands and metamorphic rocks. Other localities include northern Italy, Zaire, and Kenya. Topazolite crystals are found in the Swiss and Italian Alps in metamorphic rocks. Melanite is found in metamorphic rocks and volcanic lavas; fine crystals are found on the island of Elba (Italy), and in France and Germany.

high fire gives flashes of colour •

**BRILLIANT-CUT DEMANTOID**

Demantoid garnet has inclusions of fine, hair-like asbestos fibres, known as "horsetails".

"horsetail" inclusions •

typically worn facet edges due to softness of demantoid •

**MIXED-CUT DEMANTOID**

**BRILLIANT-CUT DEMANTOID**

crystal face has vitreous to • metallic lustre

serpentine • matrix

demantoid • crystals

**DEMANTOID GARNET CRYSTALS IN MATRIX**

**MELANITE CRYSTAL**

typically black, • opaque stone

**BRILLIANT-CUT MELANITE**

serpentine rock •

yellowish green crust of topazolite crystals

**TOPAZOLITE CRYSTALS IN MATRIX**

| Brilliant | Brilliant | Mixed |
|---|---|---|

| SG 3.85 | RI 1.85–1.89 | DR None | Lustre Vitreous to adamantine |
|---|---|---|---|

| Crystal structure Cubic | Composition Iron sulphide | Hardness 6 |
|---|---|---|

# PYRITE

With its brassy yellow colour, pyrite is often mistaken for gold (hence its other name, fool's gold). It occurs as cubes, or as "pyritohedra", which have twelve faces, each with five edges. Pyrite has been used in jewellery for thousands of years, and examples from the ancient civilizations of the Greeks, Romans, and Incas have been found. Today it is used mainly in costume jewellery, but is brittle and requires careful cutting.
• **OCCURRENCE** Pyrite is found worldwide in igneous, metamorphic, and sedimentary rocks. Fine specimens come from Spain, Mexico, Peru, Italy, and France.
• **REMARK** The name comes from the Greek word *pyr*, meaning fire, since sparks are caused if pyrite is struck with a hammer.

*striations may occur on crystal faces*

*"pyritohedral" crystal has twelve faces*

**PYRITE CRYSTAL**

*cubic form has six square faces*

Cabochon    Polished

**PYRITE CRYSTAL**

| SG 4.90 | RI None | DR None | Lustre Metallic |
|---|---|---|---|

| Crystal structure Cubic | Composition Zinc sulphide | Hardness 3½ |
|---|---|---|

# SPHALERITE

Sphalerite, also known as blende, is an important ore of zinc. It is usually very dark brown to black in colour, but, occasionally, transparent yellowish brown or green stones are found that can be faceted. Since sphalerite is soft and has perfect cleavage, it is not suitable for jewellery, and is faceted for museums and collectors only.
• **OCCURRENCE** Sphalerite crystals are usually pseudo-octahedral in shape, forming in hydrothermal veins with other minerals, such as galena, quartz, pyrite, and calcite. Transparent, cuttable stones are found in Santander (Spain) and Mexico.
• **REMARK** In the past, sphalerite has often been confused with galena (lead sulphide), to which it is similar.

*back facets are doubled*

**OCTAGONAL STEP-CUT**

*rich, reddish brown crystals*

*worn facet edges*

*high fire shows rainbow colours*

Brilliant

Brilliant

Mixed

**BRILLIANT-CUT**

**SPHALERITE CRYSTALS IN MATRIX**

| SG 4.09 | RI 2.36–2.37 | DR None | Lustre Metallic to vitreous |
|---|---|---|---|

| Crystal structure Cubic | Composition Magnesium aluminium oxide | Hardness 8 |
|---|---|---|

# SPINEL

Spinel is found in a wide range of colours due to the presence of various impurities, and is transparent to almost opaque. Red spinel coloured by chromium and iron is the most popular, although for many years it was thought to be a variety of ruby. The orange-yellow or orange-red variety is called rubicelle (a diminutive of the French word for ruby). Blue spinel is coloured by iron, and less commonly by cobalt. Occasionally, inclusions of crystals such as magnetite or apatite may occur, and some Sri Lankan spinels may include zircon crystals surrounded by brown haloes. Star stones are rare, but when cut *en cabochon* may show 4-rayed or 6-rayed stars.

• OCCURRENCE Spinel occurs in granites and metamorphic rocks, and is often found in association with corundum. Octahedral crystals and waterworn pebbles in a wide range of colours are found in the gem gravels of Burma, Sri Lanka, and Madagascar. Other localities include Afghanistan, Pakistan, Brazil, Australia, Sweden, Italy, Turkey, the former USSR, and the USA.

• REMARK Synthetic spinel has been manufactured since 1910. It has been used to imitate diamond, or coloured to imitate stones such as aqua-marine and zircon. Blue synthetic spinel, coloured by cobalt, has been used to imitate sapphire. The name may derive from the Latin word *spina*, meaning little thorn, referring to the sharp points on some crystals.

vitreous lustre

red stones originally known as Balas rubies

OCTAGONAL MIXED-CUT

blood red stones sometimes known as ruby spinel •

OVAL BRILLIANT-CUT

step-cuts clearly visible •

pink stone • from Burma

OCTAGONAL STEP-CUT

red colour due to chromium and • iron impurities

bright red colour •

• waterworn fragments found in gem gravels of Sri Lanka

CRYSTALS AND FRAGMENTS

AGGREGATE OF
SPINEL CRYSTALS

| SG 3.60 | RI 1.71–1.73 | DR None | Lustre Vitreous |
|---|---|---|---|

6-rayed star
brought out by
• cabochon-cut

• asterism is
rare in spinel

**STAR-STONE CABOCHON**

brilliant-cut
• crown facets

• step-cut
pavilion
facets

**CUSHION MIXED-CUT**

pinkish mauve
colour •

• liquid-filled
inclusions

pale pinkish
purple stone from
Sri Lanka •

**CUSHION MIXED-CUT**

**OCTAGONAL
STEP-CUT**

blue
gahnospinel
contains zinc •

gahnospinel is
named after the
Swedish chemist,
• J.G. Gahn

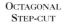

pale pinkish
• mauve colour

• synthetics have
been manufactured
since 1910

**MIXED-CUT GAHNOSPINEL**

dark, zinc-rich
• spinel crystals

**BRILLIANT-CUT
SYNTHETIC SPINEL**

Brilliant

Brilliant          Cushion

Step          Cabochon

Mixed

quartz matrix •

**SPINEL CRYSTALS
IN MATRIX**

| Crystal structure Cubic | Composition Calcium fluoride | Hardness 4 |
| --- | --- | --- |

# FLUORITE

Formerly called fluorspar, fluorite has limited use as a gemstone because it is relatively soft and therefore easily scratched. However, the wide range of colours (including yellow, blue, pink, purple, and green), the frequent incidence of more than one colour in a single specimen, and zoning or patchy distribution of colour, make it an interesting stone. Despite its fragility and perfect octahedral cleavage, stones may be faceted (usually for collectors), and can be polished very brightly. Cabochons of fluorite have been capped with rock crystal (see p.81) to protect them from scratching.

• OCCURRENCE Localities include Canada, the USA (where some of the largest crystals are found), South Africa, Thailand, Peru, Mexico, China, Poland, Hungary, Czechoslovakia, Norway, England, and Germany. Pink octa-hedral crystals are found in Switzerland. A purple and yellow banded variety called Blue John occurs in Derbyshire (England).

• REMARK The Ancient Egyptians used fluorite in statues and to carve scarabs, and the Chinese have used it in carvings for more than 300 years. In the 18th century, fluorite was powdered in water to relieve the symptoms associated with kidney disease.

bright golden
• yellow colour

• stones are
faceted for
collectors only

OCTAGONAL STEP-CUT

iron ore
matrix •

golden yellow
cubic fluorite
crystals •

FLUORITE CRYSTALS
IN MATRIX

fluorite is
soft and
difficult
• to facet

twinned
crystals •

green cubic
• crystals

pale bluish
green colour

OCTAGONAL STEP-CUT

FLUORITE CRYSTALS
IN MATRIX

black hematite
• inclusions

fluorite may be
mistaken for
glass, feldspar,
beryl, or quartz •

colourless
cubic
crystals •

CUSHION FANCY-CUT

FLUORITE
CRYSTALS IN MATRIX

| SG 3.18 | RI 1.43 | DR None | Lustre Vitreous |
| --- | --- | --- | --- |

pale pink colour

specks of black hematite

**CUSHION STEP-CUT**

tiny, white quartz crystals

cubic fluorite crystals

**FLUORITE CRYSTALS IN MATRIX**

cut stones may be highly polished and bright

mauve, cubic fluorite crystals

white quartz crystals

**OCTAGONAL STEP-CUT**

**FLUORITE CRYSTALS INTERGROWN WITH QUARTZ**

yellow and purple colour banding

smooth cleavage surface

massive habit

purple and yellow banding

green and purple banding

**CLEAVED FLUORITE CRYSTAL**

**FLUORITE ROUGH**

**BLUE JOHN VASE**
This attractive banded variety of fluorite has been carved since Roman times. The Ancient Romans believed that drinking alcohol from a cup made of Blue John would allow the drinker to imbibe without becoming drunk.

Cushion

Step

Mixed

Cameo

| Crystal structure Cubic | Composition Sodium aluminium silicate | Hardness 5½ |
|---|---|---|

# SODALITE

Sodalite, whose name reflects its sodium content, is found in all shades of blue, and is a major constituent of the rock lapis lazuli (opposite), so the two are easily confused. However, unlike lapis lazuli, sodalite very rarely contains brassy pyrite specks, and has a lower specific gravity. Sodalite may contain white streaks of the mineral calcite, and can be carved for use in jewellery.

• **OCCURRENCE** Sodalite is usually found as masses in igneous rocks. Crystals are very rare, but twelve-sided crystals have been found in the lavas of the volcano Vesuvius in Italy, although they are too small to be used in jewellery. Other localities include Brazil, Canada, India, Namibia, and the USA.

• **REMARK** The most important commercial source of sodalite is Bancroft in Ontario (Canada). It was discovered during a royal visit by Princess Margaret of England. For this reason, sodalite from Bancroft is sometimes called Princess Blue.

*white calcite patches*

*vitreous lustre*

CABOCHON

*semi-translucent stone*

*white patches of calcite*

*veins of calcite*

OVAL BRILLIANT-CUT

*uneven fracture*

POLISHED SODALITE

SODALITE ROUGH

Cabochon     Cameo

| SG 2.27 | RI 1.48 (mean) | DR None | Lustre Vitreous to greasy |
|---|---|---|---|

| Crystal structure Cubic | Composition Complex silicate | Hardness 6 |
|---|---|---|

# HAUYNE

Hauyne forms part of lapis lazuli (opposite). Intergrown with other minerals, it is seldom found as individual crystals. Hauyne has perfect cleavage, making cutting difficult, so it is faceted primarily for collectors.

• **OCCURRENCE** Hauyne is found as small, rounded grains in volcanic rocks. Ancient volcanoes of Germany and Morocco are the best-known sources.

*faceted stones are typically small*

BRILLIANT-CUT

*patches of crystals form in matrix*

*lilac hauyne crystals*

*matrix*

Brilliant

HAUYNE CRYSTALS IN MATRIX

| SG 2.40 | RI 1.50 (mean) | DR None | Lustre Vitreous to greasy |
|---|---|---|---|

| Crystal structure Various | Composition Rock containing lazurite and other minerals | Hardness 5½ |
|---|---|---|

# LAPIS LAZULI

Lapis lazuli is a blue rock made up of several different minerals, including lazurite, sodalite, hauyne, calcite, and pyrite. The composition and colour of lapis lazuli varies, but it is the intense dark blue, with minor patches of white calcite and brassy yellow pyrite, that is considered to be the best quality.

• OCCURRENCE Lapis lazuli is usually found as boulders or within limestones. The best-quality lapis lazuli is from Afghanistan, and has been used in many famous pieces, including the mask of Tutankhamun. Argentinian lapis lazuli is also of a high quality. A pale blue variety occurs in the former USSR and in Chile. Lapis lazuli from the USA is a darker shade of blue; Canadian specimens are lighter blue.

• REMARK Lapis lazuli has been worn in the belief that it will protect the wearer from evil. It has been imitated by stained jasper, and by paste with inclusions of copper. Imitation lapis lazuli is also produced by Pierre Gilson in France, and has a very similar composition to natural lapis lazuli.

BEAD NECKLACE
Specks of pyrite and streaks of calcite are visible in these lapis lazuli beads.

pale patches of calcite

brassy pyrite

BUDDHA CARVING
This carving is made from the highest quality lapis lazuli from Afghanistan.

main ingredient of imitation stone is lazurite

brassy pyrite specks

imitation stone is softer than natural lapis lazuli

GILSON IMITATION CABOCHON

GILSON IMITATION SLAB

veins of brassy pyrite

uneven fracture

blue colour due to presence of lazurite

streaks of calcite

rock is sawn open and ground with grits to give flat surface

POLISHED LAPIS LAZULI SLAB

Cabochon     Cameo     Polished

uneven fracture

LAPIS LAZULI ROUGH

| SG 2.80 | RI 1.50 (mean) | DR None | Lustre Vitreous to greasy |
|---|---|---|---|

| Crystal structure Tetragonal | Composition Calcium tungstate | Hardness 5 |
|---|---|---|

# SCHEELITE

Scheelite is quite soft and is therefore faceted only for collectors of the unusual. It has high dispersion and good fire, and varies in colour from a pale yellowish white to brown. Colourless synthetic scheelite is used to imitate diamond, but can be distinguished by its birefringence. It may also be coloured by trace metals in order to imitate other gemstones.

• **OCCURRENCE** Scheelite is found in pegmatites and metamorphic rocks. Very large crystals over 0.5kg (1lb) have been collected in Brazil, but, generally, larger crystals are not sufficiently transparent to be faceted. Other localities include Australia, Italy, Switzerland, Sri Lanka, Finland, France, and England.

*good fire •*

*• scratches show stone is soft and easily damaged*

*corners cut off to avoid • chipping*

**BRILLIANT-CUT**

*creamy yellow scheelite crystals •*

*grey magnetite matrix •*

**SQUARE STEP-CUT**

**SCHEELITE CRYSTALS IN MATRIX**

Brilliant    Step    Mixed

| SG 6.10 | RI 1.92–1.93 | DR 0.017 | Lustre Vitreous to adamantine |
|---|---|---|---|

| Crystal structure Tetragonal | Composition Tin oxide | Hardness 6½ |
|---|---|---|

# CASSITERITE

Cassiterite is the principal ore of tin. It is usually recovered from mines as black opaque grains, which are of little use in jewellery. Crystals are generally short, stubby prisms. Occasionally, rare, transparent, reddish brown crystals with adamantine lustre are found, and faceted for collectors. They could be confused with diamond, brown zircon, and sphene, but for the higher specific gravity and distinct dichroism.

• **OCCURRENCE** Cassiterite occurs in pegmatites and can be washed into alluvial deposits. Localities include the Malay Peninsula, England, Germany, Australia, Bolivia, Mexico, and Namibia.

• **REMARK** The name "cassiterite" comes from the Greek word, *kassiteros*, meaning tin.

*• double images of rear facets visible*

*colourless stone with yellowish tinge •*

**OVAL BRILLIANT-CUT**

*• rare, transparent, reddish brown stone*

*black mineral • inclusions*

*opaque, short, prismatic • crystals*

**ROUND BRILLIANT-CUT**

Brilliant    Mixed

**CASSITERITE CRYSTALS IN MATRIX**

| SG 6.95 | RI 2.00–2.10 | DR 0.100 | Lustre Adamantine |
|---|---|---|---|

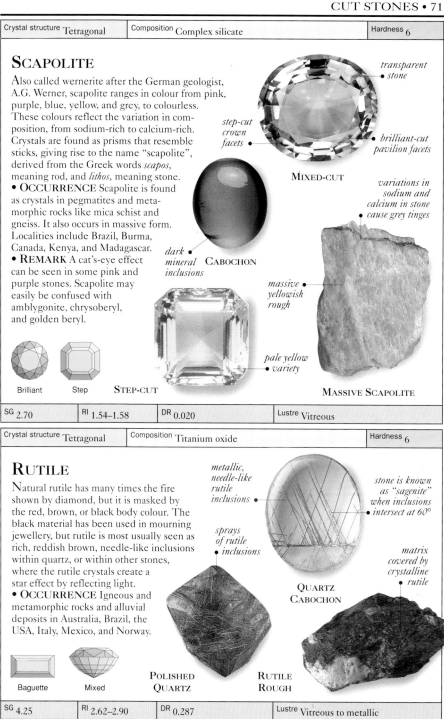

| Crystal structure Tetragonal | Composition Complex silicate | | Hardness 6 |
|---|---|---|---|

# SCAPOLITE

Also called wernerite after the German geologist, A.G. Werner, scapolite ranges in colour from pink, purple, blue, yellow, and grey, to colourless. These colours reflect the variation in composition, from sodium-rich to calcium-rich. Crystals are found as prisms that resemble sticks, giving rise to the name "scapolite", derived from the Greek words *scapos*, meaning rod, and *lithos*, meaning stone.
• OCCURRENCE Scapolite is found as crystals in pegmatites and metamorphic rocks like mica schist and gneiss. It also occurs in massive form. Localities include Brazil, Burma, Canada, Kenya, and Madagascar.
• REMARK A cat's-eye effect can be seen in some pink and purple stones. Scapolite may easily be confused with amblygonite, chrysoberyl, and golden beryl.

*transparent stone*

*step-cut crown facets*

*brilliant-cut pavilion facets*

MIXED-CUT

*variations in sodium and calcium in stone cause grey tinges*

*dark mineral inclusions* CABOCHON

*massive yellowish rough*

*pale yellow variety*

Brilliant  Step  STEP-CUT

MASSIVE SCAPOLITE

| SG 2.70 | RI 1.54–1.58 | DR 0.020 | Lustre Vitreous |
|---|---|---|---|

| Crystal structure Tetragonal | Composition Titanium oxide | | Hardness 6 |
|---|---|---|---|

# RUTILE

Natural rutile has many times the fire shown by diamond, but it is masked by the red, brown, or black body colour. The black material has been used in mourning jewellery, but rutile is most usually seen as rich, reddish brown, needle-like inclusions within quartz, or within other stones, where the rutile crystals create a star effect by reflecting light.
• OCCURRENCE Igneous and metamorphic rocks and alluvial deposits in Australia, Brazil, the USA, Italy, Mexico, and Norway.

*metallic, needle-like rutile inclusions*

*stone is known as "sagenite" when inclusions intersect at 60°*

*sprays of rutile inclusions*

*matrix covered by crystalline rutile*

QUARTZ CABOCHON

Baguette  Mixed  POLISHED QUARTZ  RUTILE ROUGH

| SG 4.25 | RI 2.62–2.90 | DR 0.287 | Lustre Vitreous to metallic |
|---|---|---|---|

| Crystal structure Tetragonal | Composition Zirconium silicate | Hardness 7½ |
|---|---|---|

# ZIRCON

Zircon is most famous for its colourless stones, which closely resemble diamonds and have been used both intentionally and mistakenly in their place. Although colourless when pure, impurities will produce yellow, orange, blue, red, brown, and green varieties. Brown stones from Thailand, Vietnam, and Kampuchea are usually heat-treated to change them into the colourless or blue stones popular in jewellery. Blue stones that revert to brown will regain the blue if reheated. Blue zircon reheated in the presence of oxygen will change to golden-yellow. Zircon may be distinguished from diamond by its double refraction and by wear and tear on its facet edges. It has been imitated by both colourless glass and synthetic spinel. Some zircon contains radioactive thorium and uranium, which eventually break down the crystal structure. Decayed stones are known as "low" zircon, with a "metamict" structure; undamaged material is "high" zircon.
• OCCURRENCE Gem-quality crystals are usually found as pebbles in alluvial deposits. Sri Lanka has been a source of gem material for over 2,000 years; other localities include Burma, Thailand, Cambodia, Vietnam, Kampuchea, Australia, Brazil, Nigeria, Tanzania, and France.
• REMARK Zircon was believed to provide the wearer with wisdom, honour, and riches, and loss of lustre was said to warn of danger. The name is from the Arabic *zargun*, which derives from the Persian for "gold colour".

• *colourless zircon produced by heating reddish brown material*

RECTANGULAR STEP-CUT

*green stones are often decayed* • *"low" zircon*

*waterworn pebble with polished* • *surface*

OVAL BRILLIANT-CUT

GREEN "METAMICT" PEBBLE

*natural golden* • *yellow colour*

OVAL MIXED-CUT

*zircon crystals* •

*golden brown is most popular colour for zircon jewellery*

*pegmatite matrix* •

*dark biotite mica* •

CUSHION BRILLIANT-CUT

CRYSTALS IN MATRIX

| SG 4.69 | RI 1.93–1.98 | DR 0.059 | Lustre Resinous to adamantine |
|---|---|---|---|

doubling of back facets

ROUND BRILLIANT-CUT

stone heat-treated to achieve blue colour

uneven colour distribution

yellowish reflections

smooth surface

ROUND BRILLIANT-CUT

WATERWORN PEBBLES

green zircon may have "metamict" structure

doubling of back facets

untreated reddish brown colour

dark golden brown stone

RECTANGULAR STEP-CUT

crown facets

CUSHION BRILLIANT-CUT

double, pyramidal ends

ZIRCON FINGER RINGS
Its adamantine lustre, strong birefringence, hardness, and vast colour range make zircon an attractive stone when set in a ring. Unfortunately, cut stones are somewhat brittle and are susceptible to damage if not treated with care.

square cross-section

leaf-green mixed-cut zircon

TETRAGONAL ZIRCON CRYSTAL

yellow zircon in centre, flanked by pale blue-violet stones

Brilliant    Cushion    Zircon    Baguette    Mixed

| Crystal structure Tetragonal | Composition Calcium aluminium silicate | Hardness 6½ |
|---|---|---|

# VESUVIANITE

This mineral was first discovered on the Italian volcano, Vesuvius, as small, perfect crystals. Also called idocrase, it may be red, yellow, green, brown, or purple. It is seldom used in jewellery, but it may be cut for collectors. Crystals are usually thick prisms with a square cross-section.
• OCCURRENCE There are several varieties: californite from California (USA) is green; rare, blue cyprine is found in Norway; yellowish green xanthite is from New York (USA); green wiluite crystals are from the former USSR. Other localities include Austria, Canada, Italy, and Switzerland.
• REMARK Vesuvianite may be confused with demantoid garnet, diopside, epidote, smoky quartz, tourmaline, zircon, and peridot.

*polished massive material*

*yellowish green variety*

CUSHION-CUT

*striations parallel to length of crystal*

*adamantine lustre*

CALIFORNITE CABOCHON

*tetragonal prism with smooth faces*

Brilliant    Step    Mixed

VESUVIANITE CRYSTAL

VESUVIANITE CRYSTALS

| SG 3.40 | RI 1.70–1.75 | DR 0.005 | Lustre Vitreous to adamantine |
|---|---|---|---|

| Crystal structure Tetragonal | Composition Sodium aluminium beryllium silicate | Hardness 6 |
|---|---|---|

# TUGTUPITE

Tugtupite was first discovered in 1960 in Greenland, where it is carved for jewellery. Colours include dark red to bright pink, and shades of orange. It may look mottled. When it is placed in the dark, the paler parts of the rock fade to white, but exposure to light restores the colour.
• OCCURRENCE Tugtupite is found as massive opaque material in pegmatite veins. It also occurs in northern Russia.
• REMARK The name derives from its occurrence in Tugtup, Greenland, and means reindeer stone.

*white albite feldspar associated with tugtupite*

*deep pink brought out by polishing surface*

*pink tugtupite*

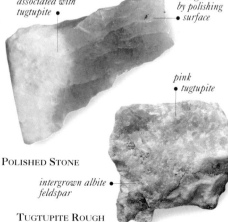

POLISHED STONE

*intergrown albite feldspar*

TUGTUPITE ROUGH

Cabochon    Cameo    Polished

| SG 2.40 | RI 1.49–1.50 | DR 0.006 | Lustre Vitreous |
|---|---|---|---|

| Crystal structure Hexagonal | Composition Beryllium aluminium silicate | Hardness 7½ |
|---|---|---|

# EMERALD (BERYL)

Emerald derives its beautiful green colour from the presence of chromium and vanadium. Emeralds are rarely flawless, so stones are often oiled to fill and disguise cracks, hide flaws, and enhance colour. To minimize the loss of material, the step-cut (or "emerald-cut", as it is known) is commonly used, but ancient engravings are known, and cameos, intaglios, and beads can make the best of a flawed stone.

• OCCURRENCE Found in granites, pegmatites, and schists, as well as alluvial deposits, the finest emeralds are from Colombia. Other sources are Austria, India, Australia, Brazil, South Africa, Egypt, the USA, Norway, Pakistan, and Zimbabwe.

• REMARK Most emeralds used in historical jewellery would have been from Cleopatra's mines in Egypt, which now yield only poor-quality emeralds.

*inclusions make stone look cloudy*

Tremolite inclusions may be found in emeralds as short rods or long fibres.

PENDELOQUE

*unusual domed front*

*stone is semi-translucent*

*group of inclusions*

OCTAGONAL CABOCHON

POLISHED PEBBLE

Synthetic emeralds have characteristic veil or wisp-like, liquid-filled inclusions.

*cracks and inclusions common in emerald*

*brilliant-cut crown facets*

MIXED-CUT

*scratched prism face*

*good emerald-green colour*

*prism has flat ends*

SYNTHETIC PENDELOQUE

HEXAGONAL CRYSTAL

*crystals often found worn or etched*

*white calcite crystals*

CRYSTAL IN MATRIX

| Pendeloque | Step | Step | Cabochon |
|---|---|---|---|

| SG 2.71 | RI 1.57–1.58 | DR 0.006 | Lustre Vitreous |
|---|---|---|---|

| Crystal structure Hexagonal | Composition Beryllium aluminium silicate | Hardness 7½ |
|---|---|---|

# AQUAMARINE (BERYL)

In the 19th century the preferred colour for aquamarine was sea-green, and indeed the name itself means sea water. Today the most valued colours are sky-blue and dark blue. Aquamarine is dichroic, appearing blue or colourless as the stone is viewed from different angles. Gem-quality aquamarine is found as hexagonal crystals, which may be up to 1m (39in) long and flawless, with striations along the length of the crystal. Aquamarine is often cut with the table facet parallel to the length of the crystal in order to emphasize the deepest coloration.

• OCCURRENCE The best of the gem-quality aquamarine is found in Brazil, where it occurs in pegmatites and alluvial deposits of gravel, locally called *cascalho*. Other localities include the Urals (Russia), Afghanistan, Pakistan, India, and, more recently exploited, Nigeria. A dark blue variety occurs in Madagascar.

• REMARK Almost all aquamarine in the market has been heat-treated to enhance its colour. Care must be taken not to overheat the stones, as they may become colourless.

*untreated, sky-blue stone* •

OCTAGONAL STEP-CUT

*cat's-eye effect visible on cabochon* •

*fibrous habit* •

CABOCHON

*step-cut typical for aquamarine* •

*heat-treatment has lightened colour* •

OCTAGONAL STEP-CUT

*untreated stone has greenish tinge* •

OCTAGONAL STEP-CUT

*many small facets* •

BRILLIANT-CUT

*poor-quality, flawed stone* •

*popular aquamarine colour* •

*crystal is too green and will require heat-treatment* •

AQUAMARINE CRYSTALS

Brilliant          Step          Cabochon

| SG 2.69 | RI 1.57–1.58 | DR 0.006 | Lustre Vitreous |
|---|---|---|---|

| Crystal structure Hexagonal | Composition Beryllium aluminium silicate | Hardness 7½ |
|---|---|---|

# HELIODOR (BERYL)

*glowing, golden yellow colour*

Heliodor, a yellow or golden yellow form of beryl, has always been linked with the Sun. Gem-quality specimens are occasionally found, but more usually inclusions of fine, slender tubes are present, which are visible to the naked eye.
• OCCURRENCE Heliodor is found associated with aquamarine in granitic pegmatites. The best-quality stones are found in the Urals (Russia). Brazilian heliodor is often a pale yellow and is step-cut to give depth of colour. Heliodor from Madagascar is a finer colour. Other localities include the Ukraine, Namibia, and the USA.

*heart-shaped cut keeps maximum possible weight*

**SCISSORS-CUT**

*bevel-edged crystal with flat ends*

Marquise   Table   Baguette

**FANCY-CUT**

**HELIODOR CRYSTALS IN MATRIX**

| SG 2.80 | RI 1.57–1.58 | DR 0.005 | Lustre Vitreous |
|---|---|---|---|

| Crystal structure Hexagonal | Composition Beryllium aluminium silicate | Hardness 7½ |
|---|---|---|

# GOSHENITE (BERYL)

*stones are transparent*

Goshenite is the pure, colourless variety of beryl. It has been used to imitate diamond or emerald, by placing silver or green-coloured metal foil behind a cut goshenite gemstone, then placing the stone in a closed setting so that the foil cannot be detected.
• OCCURRENCE Goshenite is named after Goshen, Massachusetts, in the USA, where it was first found. Present localities include Canada, Brazil, and the former USSR.
• REMARK Pale and colourless beryl was once used for the lenses in spectacles, thus the German word for spectacles, *brille*, may have been derived from the word "beryl".

*vitreous lustre*

**FANCY-CUT**

*crystals have hexagonal outline*

*spiky inclusions are common*

Brilliant   Step   Mixed

**BRILLIANT-CUT**

**TABULAR CRYSTAL**

| SG 2.80 | RI 1.58–1.59 | DR 0.008 | Lustre Vitreous |
|---|---|---|---|

| Crystal structure Hexagonal | Composition Beryllium aluminium silicate | Hardness 7½ |
|---|---|---|

# MORGANITE (BERYL)

Coloured by manganese impurities, the pink, rose, peach, and violet varieties of beryl are called morganite, after the American banker and gem enthusiast, J. Pierpoint Morgan. Morganite tends to occur as short and stubby (tabular) prisms, and is dichroic, showing either two shades of the body colour, or one shade and colourless.

• OCCURRENCE The first morganite to be described was a pale rose-coloured specimen from California (USA), where it occurred with tourmaline. Some of the finest morganite is from Madagascar; Brazil produces pure pink crystals, as well as some containing aquamarine and morganite in the same crystal. Other localities include Elba (Italy), Mozambique, Namibia, Zimbabwe, and (recently discovered) Pakistan.

• REMARK Stones with a yellow or orange tinge may be heat-treated for a purer pink.

typical pale pink colour

many small facets

OVAL MIXED-CUT

BRILLIANT-CUT

vitreous lustre

DROP-SHAPED CUT

pink colour from manganese

liquid-filled inclusions

ROUND BRILLIANT-CUT

Brilliant    Step

MORGANITE ROUGH

| SG 2.80 | RI 1.58–1.59 | DR 0.008 | Lustre Vitreous |
|---|---|---|---|

| Crystal structure Hexagonal | Composition Beryllium aluminium silicate | Hardness 7½ |
|---|---|---|

# RED BERYL

Very rare, and seldom seen as a cut stone, red beryl nonetheless has an unusually intense colour, due to the presence of manganese.

• OCCURRENCE Found in rhyolites in the Thomas Mountains and Wah Wah Mountains in Utah in the USA.

• REMARK Red beryl is also called bixbite (not to be confused with bixbyite, a manganese-iron oxide).

prismatic red beryl crystal

rhyolite matrix

Brilliant

CRYSTAL IN MATRIX

| SG 2.80 | RI 1.58–1.59 | DR 0.008 | Lustre Vitreous |
|---|---|---|---|

| Crystal structure Hexagonal | Composition Calcium phosphate | Hardness 5 |

# APATITE

With a value of only 5 on the Mohs scale of hardness, apatite is seldom faceted as a gemstone, except for collectors. However, when cut correctly, stones are bright with strong colours. Transparent to opaque, apatite occurs as colourless, yellow, blue, violet, or green hexagonal prisms or tabular crystals.
• OCCURRENCE Apatite is an abundant mineral, found in many types of rock, but most gem-quality material is associated with pegmatites. Blue Burmese apatite is strongly dichroic, and shows colourless or blue when viewed from different directions. Fibrous blue apatite from Burma and Sri Lanka may be cut *en cabochon* to show a cat's-eye. Chatoyant stones are also found in Brazil, along with yellow, blue, and green varieties. Other localities include the Kola Peninsula (Russia), Canada, East Africa, Sweden, Spain, and Mexico.
• REMARK Spanish apatite is often called "asparagus stone", due to its yellowish green colour.

• blue-grey fibrous apatite

chipped facet edge, due to brittleness • of stone

CAT'S-EYE CABOCHON

• black inclusions

ROUND BRILLIANT-CUT

OCTAGONAL STEP-CUT

• grey-green colour

OCTAGONAL STEP-CUT

stones are opaque • to transparent

CUSHION MIXED-CUT

• cut stones are bright and strongly coloured

RECTANGULAR STEP-CUT

• pyramidal end

• yellow hexagonal prism

colourless apatite crystal •

APATITE CRYSTAL

| Baguette | Step |

quartz • and gibertite matrix

APATITE CRYSTALS IN MATRIX

| Step | Cabochon |

| SG 3.20 | RI 1.63–1.64 | DR 0.003 | Lustre Vitreous |

| Crystal structure Hexagonal | Composition Beryllium magnesium aluminium oxide | Hardness 8 |
|---|---|---|

# TAAFFEITE

Taaffeite is very rare, and is unique in being the only gemstone not recognized as a new mineral species until it had been faceted. The first specimen (see right) was found by Count Taaffe in Ireland, in a jeweller's box of stones. It looked like spinel, had a pale mauve tinge, and was cushion-cut, but was eventually found to be a new, doubly refractive (rather than singly refractive like spinel) mineral. Since then, more specimens have been found; these range in hue from red to blue to almost colourless.

• OCCURRENCE Taaffeite occurs in Sri Lanka, China, and the former USSR.

• REMARK No imitation taaffeites appear to exist.

• *first specimen to be identified*

• *greyish mauve colour*

**CUSHION-CUT**

*transparent stone* •

*semi-translucent pebble* •

*vitreous lustre* •

**ROUND BRILLIANT-CUT**

**TAAFFEITE ROUGH**

| Brilliant | Brilliant | Cushion |
|---|---|---|

| SG 3.61 | RI 1.72–1.77 | DR 0.004 | Lustre Vitreous |
|---|---|---|---|

| Crystal structure Hexagonal | Composition Barium titanium silicate | Hardness 6½ |
|---|---|---|

# BENITOITE

The blue crystals of benitoite were only discovered in 1906, by a mineral prospector who mistook them for sapphires. Crystals are shaped like flattened triangles, and have a strong dispersion similar to diamond, but this is masked by the colour. Dichroism is strong: the stone appears blue or colourless when viewed from different angles. Colourless crystals occur, but are rarely faceted.

• OCCURRENCE Crystals occur in veins in blue schists. The sole source is in San Benito County, California (USA), after which the stone is named.

*appears colourless at certain angles* •

**BRILLIANT-CUT**

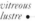

• *unevenly distributed colour*

**BRILLIANT-CUT**

*pyramidal end* •

*conchoidal fracture* •

*blue benitoite crystals* •

**BENITOITE CRYSTAL FRAGMENT**

**BENITOITE CRYSTALS IN MATRIX**

| Brilliant | Brilliant | Cushion |
|---|---|---|

| SG 3.67 | RI 1.76–1.80 | DR 0.047 | Lustre Vitreous |
|---|---|---|---|

| Crystal structure Trigonal | Composition Silicon dioxide | Hardness 7 |
|---|---|---|

# ROCK CRYSTAL (QUARTZ)

Colourless and transparent, rock crystal is the most widely distributed variety of quartz, one of the most common minerals of the Earth's crust. The crystals are usually found as colourless hexagonal prisms, with pyramidal ends and striations perpendicular to their length; they are often twinned. Cleavage is poor and fracture conchoidal.
• OCCURRENCE Although found worldwide, the most important sources of rock crystal are in Brazil. Other localities include the Swiss and French Alps, where fine crystals occur, and Madagascar, the former USSR, and the USA.
• REMARK The name "quartz" comes from the Greek word *krustallos*, meaning ice, because it was thought that quartz was ice formed by the gods. Since the Middle Ages, crystal balls made of rock crystal have been used to predict the future. Today, rock crystal is used in lamps, lenses, and the manufacture of glass and precision instruments. Synthetic rock crystal has been produced since 1950 for use in watches.

*transparent stone* •

*facet edges may wear on older stones* •

**ROUND BRILLIANT-CUT**

• *vitreous lustre*

**CUSHION BRILLIANT-CUT**

*carved grooves* •

*drilled hole* •

**POLISHED BEAD**

**POLISHED ROCK CRYSTAL**
This flat disc of polished rock crystal has been engraved, and set with an enamelled monogram of blue, black, and gold.

*colourless through to yellowish shading* •

*striations on prism faces* •

*hexagonal crystals* •

*pyramidal ends* •

Bead

Cameo

Brilliant

Step

**SINGLE CRYSTAL**

**CRYSTALS**

| SG 2.65 | RI 1.54–1.55 | DR 0.009 | Lustre Vitreous |
|---|---|---|---|

| Crystal structure Trigonal | Composition Silicon dioxide | Hardness 7 |
|---|---|---|

# AMETHYST (QUARTZ)

Crystalline quartz in shades of purple, lilac, or mauve is called amethyst, a stone traditionally worn to guard against drunkenness, and to instil a sober and serious mind. Amethyst is dichroic, showing a bluish or reddish purple tinge when viewed from different angles. Usually faceted as a mixed- or step-cut, amethyst has distinctive inclusions which look like tiger-stripes, thumb-prints, or feathers. Some amethyst is heat-treated to change the colour to yellow, producing citrine (see opposite). Crystals that are part citrine and part amethyst are called ametrine.

• OCCURRENCE Amethyst is found in alluvial deposits or in geodes. Some of the largest geodes containing amethyst are in Brazil. Amethyst from the Urals (Russia) has a reddish tinge; Canadian amethyst is violet. Other localities include Sri Lanka, India, Uruguay, Madagascar, the USA, Germany, Australia, Namibia, and Zambia.

• REMARK Poor-quality material is often tumbled to make beads. If a stone is pale it may be set in a closed setting or have foil placed behind it to enhance the colour. Amethyst has been imitated by glass and synthetic corundum.

Characteristic tiger-stripe inclusions are caused by parallel, liquid-filled canals.

**TIE-PIN**
Amethyst jewellery was popular in the late 19th century. This handsome gold tie-pin is adorned with an octagonal step-cut amethyst.

typical •
purplish
violet
colour

**OVAL MIXED-CUT**

purple stone
• from Russia

• polished,
convex
front

alternate colours
due to twinning •

colour darkens
towards tip of
• amethyst crystal

**HEXAGONAL
MIXED-CUT**

slice cut •
perpendicular
to length of
crystal

**AMETHYST CRYSTAL SLICE**

**AMETHYST CRYSTALS
ASSOCIATED WITH
ROCK CRYSTAL**

Baguette    Bead    Mixed

| SG 2.65 | RI 1.54–1.55 | DR 0.009 | Lustre Vitreous |
|---|---|---|---|

| Crystal structure Trigonal | Composition Silicon dioxide | Hardness 7 |
| --- | --- | --- |

# CITRINE (QUARTZ)

Citrine is the yellow or golden yellow variety of quartz. The yellow coloration, due to the presence of iron, is also responsible for the name, derived from the word "citrus". Natural citrine is usually a pale yellow, but rare; most citrine on the market is heat-treated amethyst (see opposite).

• OCCURRENCE Gem-quality citrine is extremely rare. The best material is found in Brazil, Spain, Madagascar, and the former USSR.

• REMARK Citrine has been used to imitate topaz (see pp.106–107), and was once called Brazilian topaz.

*orange tinge often seen in citrine •*

MIXED-CUT

*• yellow colour due to presence of iron*

*pyramidal end •*

Brilliant   Pendeloque   Cabochon

MIXED-CUT
PENDELOQUE

CITRINE CRYSTAL

| SG 2.65 | RI 1.54–1.55 | DR 0.009 | Lustre Vitreous |
| --- | --- | --- | --- |

| Crystal structure Trigonal | Composition Silicon dioxide | Hardness 7 |
| --- | --- | --- |

# ROSE QUARTZ

Pink or peach-coloured quartz is called rose quartz, and is mainly used in decorative carvings. Its colour is thought to be due to the presence of small amounts of titanium. Crystals of rose quartz are very rare; more usually, massive lumps are found, which can be carved, or cut *en cabochon* or as beads. Transparent material is uncommon; it is usually cloudy or cracked, partly because it is so brittle. Rutile inclusions in rose quartz may produce a star effect when the stone is cut *en cabochon*.

• OCCURRENCE Rose quartz is found in pegmatites. The best material is from Madagascar, but Brazil produces a greater quantity. Other sites are Scotland, the former USSR, Colorado (USA), and Spain.

ROSE QUARTZ SEAL
Intaglio seals such as this, made with an incised rather than a raised design, were very popular in Ancient Rome.

*• pale pink stone from Madagascar*

*rose quartz crystals •*

BRILLIANT-CUT

*crystals are typically cloudy •*

Bead        Mixed        Cameo

ROSE QUARTZ
CRYSTALS

| SG 2.65 | RI 1.54–1.55 | DR 0.009 | Lustre Vitreous |
| --- | --- | --- | --- |

| Crystal structure Trigonal | Composition Silicon dioxide | Hardness 7 |
|---|---|---|

# BROWN QUARTZ

Brown quartz includes quartz of a light brown or dark brown colour, greyish brown "smoky" quartz, and the black variety called morion. Brown or smoky quartz from the Cairngorm Mountains of Scotland is called cairngorm. When irradiated, colourless quartz may change colour to greyish brown, suggesting that brown quartz may have been formed by natural radiation within the ground. Brown quartz crystals are hexagonal prisms with pyramidal ends, in which inclusions of the mineral rutile may be present.
• OCCURRENCE Crystals weighing as much as 300kg (650lb) have been found in Brazil. Other localities include Madagascar, the Swiss Alps, Colorado (USA), Australia, and Spain.
• REMARK Much of the smoky quartz on the market is in fact irradiated rock crystal. Brown quartz has been confused with andalusite, axinite, idocrase, and brown tourmaline.

colour may be due to natural irradiation

FANCY-CUT SMOKY QUARTZ

vitreous lustre

characteristic greyish brown colour

BRILLIANT-CUT SMOKY QUARTZ

**SNUFF BOTTLE**
Like most varieties of quartz, smoky quartz may be polished and fashioned in many ways. This snuff bottle, with red stopper and spoon, is of Chinese origin.

pyramidal end

opaque hexagonal prism

horizontal striations on prism face

MORION CRYSTAL

incised image

**INTAGLIO SEAL**
This incised intaglio was carved in smoky quartz, and has been set in a polished oval of obsidian, a natural volcanic glass. Intaglio seals were popular with the Ancient Romans, and this piece depicts a Roman wearing a helmet.

polishing of one facet makes interior visible

Mixed    Cameo

smoky quartz intaglio

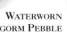

WATERWORN CAIRNGORM PEBBLE

| SG 2.65 | RI 1.54–1.55 | DR 0.009 | Lustre Vitreous |
|---|---|---|---|

| Crystal structure Trigonal | Composition Silicon dioxide | Hardness 7 |
|---|---|---|

# AVENTURINE QUARTZ

This form of quartz contains inclusions of small crystals that reflect light, and which give a range of colours – depending on the nature of the inclusion. Green aventurine quartz has platy inclusions of green fuchsite mica; pyrite inclusions give a brown colour; a greenish brown variety may be due to the mineral goethite. Other inclusions give bluish white, bluish green, or orange varieties.

• OCCURRENCE Aventurine quartz is found in Brazil, India, and Russia. Other localities include the USA, Japan, and Tanzania.

• REMARK Aventurine quartz has been confused with aventurine feldspar, amazonite, and jade. A simulant, known as goldstone, has been made to imitate both aventurine quartz and aventurine feldspar. It contains small triangles and hexagons of copper held in glass. With a x10 hand lens it should be possible to see the outlines of the copper spangles.

brassy yellow mica inclusions •

oval, orange-brown cabochon •

CABOCHON

fuchsite mica inclusions give green colour •

The copper inclusions in goldstone are visible with a x10 hand lens.

POLISHED SLAB

cryptocrystalline quartz with light-reflecting inclusions •

AVENTURINE QUARTZ ROUGH

| Cabochon | Cameo | Polished |
|---|---|---|

| SG 2.65 | RI 1.54–1.55 | DR 0.009 | Lustre Vitreous |
|---|---|---|---|

| Crystal structure Trigonal | Composition Silicon dioxide | Hardness 7 |
|---|---|---|

# MILKY QUARTZ

This form of quartz derives its distinctive milky white or cream colour from inclusions of gas and liquid bubbles. The degree of milkiness depends on the number and size of inclusions present. Crystals are hexagonal prisms with pyramidal ends.

• OCCURRENCE Very large crystals are found in Siberia. Other localities include Brazil, the European Alps, Madagascar, the USA, and Namibia.

• REMARK When polished or cut *en cabochon*, it may be confused with opal.

milkiness due to gas and liquid inclusions •

double, pyramidal ends •

| Brilliant | Cameo |
|---|---|

OVAL CUSHION-CUT

HEXAGONAL CRYSTAL

| SG 2.65 | RI 1.54–1.55 | DR 0.009 | Lustre Vitreous |
|---|---|---|---|

| Crystal structure Trigonal | Composition Silicon dioxide | Hardness 7 |
|---|---|---|

# CHATOYANT QUARTZ

The three varieties of quartz described here all have a fibrous structure, with inclusions of crocidolite (blue asbestos) that cause a "cat's-eye" effect known as chatoyancy. This effect is best seen when the stones are cut *en cabochon*. Each stone displays different colours according to the exact nature of the inclusions. The greyish yellow, semi-translucent appearance of quartz cat's-eye is due to inclusions of crocidolite "asbestos" and, less commonly, hornblende. It has a silky lustre. Tiger's-eye is black, with iron oxide staining that gives yellow and golden brown stripes. Hawk's-eye forms when crocidolite changes to quartz, but the blue-grey or blue-green colour of the original remains.
• OCCURRENCE Quartz cat's-eye comes from Sri Lanka, India, and Brazil. The most important source of tiger's-eye is in South Africa, where it is found in thick slabs, together with the less common hawk's-eye. Chatoyant quartz is also found in Australia and the USA.
• REMARK Chatoyant quartz is always called *quartz* cat's-eye to avoid confusion with other chatoyant gems, particularly chrysoberyl.

*wavy, fibrous structure* •

*markings resemble tiger stripes* •

**TIGER'S-EYE POLISHED SLAB**

• *yellow-brown stripes due to iron oxide staining*

**POLISHED TIGER'S-EYE**

*original blue colour and fibrous structure retained* •

**HAWK'S-EYE ROUGH**

**HAWK'S-EYE CIGARETTE BOX**
In this attractive ornament, made of polished slices of blue hawk's-eye, the wavy, fibrous nature of the original asbestos can be clearly seen. Partial oxidation has created a few yellow waves.

*pale, almost colourless quartz* •

*cabochon-cut brings out cat's-eye effect* •

*waterworn fragment exhibits fibrous structure* •

**QUARTZ CAT'S-EYE CABOCHON**

*rough displays no chatoyancy* •

**QUARTZ CAT'S-EYE ROUGH**

Bead    Cabochon    Polished

| SG 2.65 | RI 1.54–1.55 | DR 0.009 | Lustre Vitreous |
|---|---|---|---|

| Crystal structure Trigonal | Composition Silicon dioxide | Hardness 7 |
|---|---|---|

# QUARTZ WITH INCLUSIONS

Quartz specimens with mineral inclusions are very common and make attractive gemstones. "Rutilated quartz" or "sagenite", popularly known as Venus-hair stone, is quartz with needle-like rutile crystals. These may be red, black, or brassy yellow, and have a metallic lustre. "Tourmalinated quartz" has inclusions of black tourmaline, which form prismatic or needle-like crystals. Opaque, metallic yellow inclusions of gold are found in specimens of "gold quartz". Inclusions of silver may also be found within quartz, often in branch-like dendrites, and are silvery grey or black, opaque, and metallic. The iron minerals, goethite and pyrite, are also found as inclusions. If cut *en cabochon*, quartz containing goethite may show the cat's-eye effect.
• OCCURRENCE Quartz with inclusions is found in Madagascar, Brazil, South Africa, India, Sri Lanka, Germany, and Switzerland.

**PERFUME BOTTLE**
This piece of quartz contains distinctive inclusions of black, needle-like tourmaline crystals. It has been shaped, hollowed out, and polished to make a bottle.

• *needle-like tourmaline inclusions*

*reddish brown rutile inclusions* •

*hexagonal quartz prisms* •

**RUTILATED QUARTZ CRYSTALS IN MATRIX**

| Brilliant | Bead | Cabochon | Cameo |
|---|---|---|---|

| SG 2.65 | RI 1.54–1.55 | DR 0.009 | Lustre Vitreous |
|---|---|---|---|

| Crystal structure Trigonal | Composition Silicon dioxide | Hardness 7 |
|---|---|---|

# FIRE AGATE (CHALCEDONY)

Fire agate belongs to the chalcedony family of microcrystalline quartzes. These are either solid-coloured stones, or have bands or moss-like or dendritic inclusions (agates). The distinctive iridescent colours of fire agate are caused by layers of iron oxide within the quartz. This rainbow effect may be brought out by cutting *en cabochon*.
• OCCURRENCE Fire agate is found in Arizona (USA) and Mexico.
• REMARK Iris quartz has a similar irides-cence, but this is caused by internal cracks.

• *iridescence brought out by cabochon-cut*

• *iron oxide inclusions give "oily" effect*

**FIRE AGATE CABOCHON**

*rainbow colours* •

**POLISHED FIRE AGATE PEBBLE**

| Bead | Cabochon | Mixed | Cameo |
|---|---|---|---|

| SG 2.61 | RI 1.53–1.54 | DR 0.004 | Lustre Vitreous |
|---|---|---|---|

| Crystal structure Trigonal | Composition Silicon dioxide | Hardness 7 |
|---|---|---|

# AGATE (CHALCEDONY)

Agate occurs in nodular masses in rocks such as volcanic lavas. When split open, they reveal an amazing variety of colours and patterns, and a distinct banding that distinguishes agate from other kinds of chalcedony (the compact, micro-crystalline variety of quartz). Band colours are determined by the differing impurities present, although, being porous, agate is often dyed or stained to enhance the natural colour. Agate also occurs in several distinct forms. Fortification agate has angularly arranged bands resembling an aerial view of a fortress. Moss agate (or mocha stone) is translucent and colourless, white or grey, with dark, moss- or tree-like (dendritic) inclusions. It is usually cut as thin slabs, or polished as ornaments, brooches, or pendants. Agatized wood is fossilized wood that has had its organic matter replaced by agate.

• OCCURRENCE Probably the most famous area for agates is Idar-Oberstein in Germany, where agate has been collected since 1548. It now imports agates from the huge deposits in Uruguay and Brazil. Moss agate occurs in the Hindustan area of India; also China and the USA. The most famous agatized wood is found in the Petrified Forest in Arizona (USA). Agates are also found in Mexico, Madagascar, Italy, Egypt, India, China, and Scotland.

*angular and wavy agate banding*

*white quartz crystals*

**STAINED AND POLISHED OVAL**

*more stain taken up in some areas*

*distinctive concentric banding*

**STAINED AND POLISHED SLICE**

*parallel bands and patterns*

*agate is often collected and polished by enthusiasts*

*agate forms in cavities in volcanic rocks*

**POLISHED SLICE**

*silica-rich fluids give colour to bands*

**AGATE ROUGH**

| SG 2.61 | RI 1.53–1.54 | DR 0.004 | Lustre Vitreous |
|---|---|---|---|

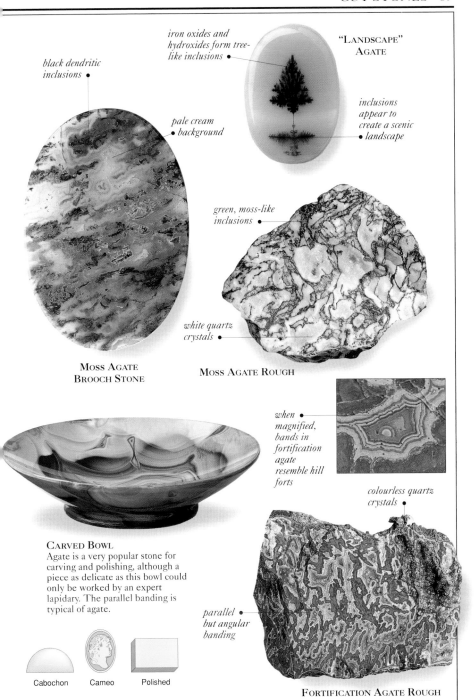

black dendritic
inclusions •

iron oxides and
hydroxides form tree-
like inclusions •

"LANDSCAPE"
AGATE

pale cream
• background

inclusions
appear to
create a scenic
• landscape

green, moss-like
inclusions •

white quartz
crystals •

MOSS AGATE
BROOCH STONE

MOSS AGATE ROUGH

when •
magnified,
bands in
fortification
agate
resemble hill
forts

colourless quartz
crystals •

**CARVED BOWL**
Agate is a very popular stone for
carving and polishing, although a
piece as delicate as this bowl could
only be worked by an expert
lapidary. The parallel banding is
typical of agate.

parallel •
but angular
banding

Cabochon    Cameo    Polished

FORTIFICATION AGATE ROUGH

| Crystal structure | Trigonal | Composition | Silicon dioxide | Hardness | 7 |
|---|---|---|---|---|---|

# ONYX, SARD, AND SARDONYX (CHALCEDONY)

Onyx, sard, and sardonyx are all varieties of the microcrystalline quartz, chalcedony. Onyx is similar to agate (see pp.88–89), but it has straight rather than curved bands. These may be brown and white or black and white. Sard is a brownish red variety, also similar to agate. Sardonyx, a blend of sard and onyx, has the straight white bands of onyx and the brownish red of sard. All three varieties are carved as small sculptures and intaglios, or may be polished, tumbled, or cut as beads. They are renowned as excellent materials for inlay work. Since Ancient Egyptian times, onyx has been stained to improve or change its colour. Much onyx has been produced by soaking agate in a sugar solution, then heating it in sulphuric acid to carbonize the sugar particles. Sard may be imitated by saturating chalcedony with an iron solution.

• **OCCURRENCE** Found worldwide, they are formed by the deposition of silica in gas cavities in lavas, which results in the distinctive bands.

• **REMARK** Onyx seals were very popular with the Romans, who carved the pattern of the seal in negative relief to give a raised print. They often used stones with several layers, each of a different colour, which were then individually carved to produce a different pattern in each layer.

**FLOWER CAMEO**
This cameo was worked from a single piece of onyx. The dark, opaque layer has been carved away in the shape of a flower to reveal the pale layer beneath.

**STRAIGHT SEAL**
The straight layers of onyx have been exposed to dramatic effect in this seal, an ornament popular with the Romans.

*straight brown and white banding, characteristic of onyx*

**ONYX WITH WHITE OPAL**

*parallel bands of different colours*

*vitreous lustre on some surfaces*

**POLISHED ONYX SLAB**

Bead

Cabochon

Polished

| SG | 2.61 | RI | 1.53–1.54 | DR | 0.004 | Lustre | Vitreous |
|---|---|---|---|---|---|---|---|

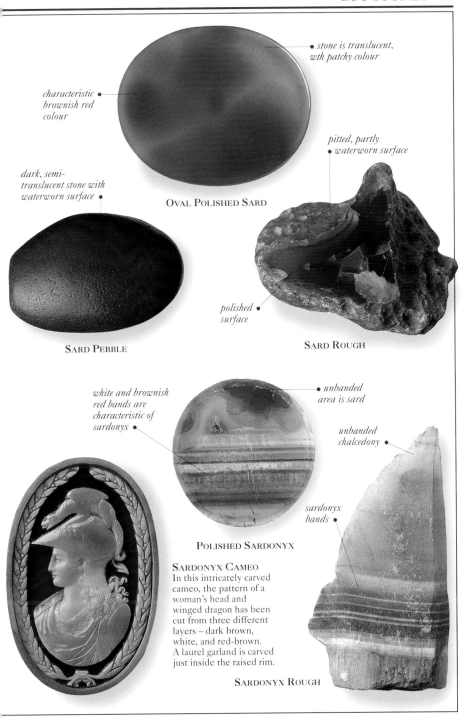

stone is translucent, wth patchy colour

characteristic brownish red colour

pitted, partly waterworn surface

**OVAL POLISHED SARD**

dark, semi-translucent stone with waterworn surface

polished surface

**SARD PEBBLE**

**SARD ROUGH**

white and brownish red bands are characteristic of sardonyx

unbanded area is sard

unbanded chalcedony

sardonyx bands

**POLISHED SARDONYX**

**SARDONYX CAMEO**
In this intricately carved cameo, the pattern of a woman's head and winged dragon has been cut from three different layers – dark brown, white, and red-brown. A laurel garland is carved just inside the raised rim.

**SARDONYX ROUGH**

| Crystal structure Trigonal | Composition Silicon dioxide | Hardness 7 |
|---|---|---|

# CHRYSOPRASE/PRASE (CHALCEDONY)

Used by both the Greeks and Romans as a decorative stone, chrysoprase, a translucent, apple-green stone, is the most valued variety of chalcedony. The colour, derived from the presence of nickel, may fade in sunlight, and stones may then be confused with fine jade (see pp.124–125).

• **OCCURRENCE** Mines in Poland and Czechoslovakia once produced very fine chrysoprase. However, since 1965 the best-quality material has come from Queensland (Australia). Other localities are the Urals (Russia), California (USA), Brazil, and Austria.

• **REMARK** Another green chalcedony, prase, has a more sombre hue and is very rare.

PRASE CAMEO
Set in gold as an ornamental pin, this piece of fine green prase has been carved and polished into a classically styled cameo.

fragments of host rock

apple-green chrysoprase

**CHRYSOPRASE ROUGH**

| Bead | Cabochon | Cameo |
|---|---|---|

| SG 2.61 | RI 1.53–1.54 | DR 0.004 | Lustre Vitreous to waxy |
|---|---|---|---|

| Crystal structure Trigonal | Composition Silicon dioxide | Hardness 7 |
|---|---|---|

# JASPER (CHALCEDONY)

Jasper is a massive, fine-grained, opaque variety of chalcedony, believed to protect against sight defects and drought. It occurs in shades of brown, greyish blue, red, yellow, and green, and mixtures of these. "Orbicular" jasper has white or grey, eye-shaped patterns surrounded by red jasper. "Riband" jasper is striped and used in carvings, cameos, and intaglios, which show off its layered structure. Hornstone is a grey variety.

• **OCCURRENCE** Red jasper occurs in India and Venezuela; various colours occur in the USA, especially orbicular jasper in California; red and green riband jasper occurs in Russia. It also occurs in France and Germany.

stone may break easily at junction of stripes

polished surface

**RIBAND JASPER FRAGMENT**

mammillated habit

iron oxide gives red colouring

white quartz vein

**RED JASPER ROUGH**

| Cameo | Polished |
|---|---|

**RED JASPER ROUGH**

| SG 2.61 | RI 1.53–1.54 | DR 0.004 | Lustre Vitreous |
|---|---|---|---|

| Crystal structure Trigonal | Composition Silicon dioxide | | Hardness 7 |
|---|---|---|---|

# CARNELIAN (CHALCEDONY)

Also called cornelian, this translucent, reddish orange variety of chalcedony was once thought to still the blood and calm the temper. Its various shades of red are due to the presence of iron oxide. Stones may be uniformly coloured or faintly banded.
• OCCURRENCE The best carnelian is from India, where it is placed in the sun to change brown tints to red.
• REMARK Most carnelian on the market is stained chalcedony from Brazil or Uruguay.

*• typical reddish orange stone from India*

*colour bands formed by iron oxide impurities •*

POLISHED STONE

POLISHED CARNELIAN FRAGMENT

Bead          Cabochon          Cameo

| SG 2.61 | RI 1.53–1.54 | DR 0.004 | Lustre Vitreous to waxy |
|---|---|---|---|

| Crystal structure Trigonal | Composition Silicon dioxide | | Hardness 7 |
|---|---|---|---|

# BLOODSTONE AND PLASMA (CHALCEDONY)

Bloodstone (also called heliotrope) and plasma are both opaque, green, spotted varieties of chalcedony, used for decorative carvings and cameos. The dark green of bloodstone is spotted with red, due to the presence of iron oxides. These distinctive spots seem to resemble blood, and give the stone its name. Plasma is also green and may have yellowish spots.
• OCCURRENCE India is the primary source of bloodstone, but it also occurs in Brazil, China, Australia, and the USA. Plasma is mined in Zimbabwe.
• REMARK In the Middle Ages, bloodstone was attributed with special powers, as the spots were thought to be the blood of Jesus Christ. In Germany, hematite is also called bloodstone, so this variety is known as bluestone.

ROMAN CAMEO
The typical red spotting in dark green bloodstone appears as an almost solid mass in the high relief of this cameo.

*• raised relief carved from red spotting*

*scattered red spots and veins •*

*polished material • often used as inlay*

*very deep • green*

Bead          Cameo          Polished

POLISHED BLOODSTONE SLAB

PLASMA ROUGH

| SG 2.61 | RI 1.53–1.54 | DR 0.004 | Lustre Vitreous |
|---|---|---|---|

| Crystal structure Trigonal | Composition Aluminium oxide | Hardness 9 |
|---|---|---|

# RUBY (CORUNDUM)

Ruby – the name given to red, gem-quality corundum – is one of the best gemstones for jewellery settings. Rubies may be any shade of red, from pinkish to purplish or brownish red, depending on the chromium and iron content of the stone. Frequent twinning of the crystals makes the material liable to fracture, yet ruby is a tough mineral, second only to diamond in hardness. Crystal prisms are hexagonal with tapering or flat ends. As the crystals grow they form new layers, and depending on the geological conditions and minerals present, colour variations, called zoning, occur.

*rubies were thought to ward off misfortune • and ill-health*

Rutile inclusions cause a silky appearance, which heat treatment will remove.

• **OCCURRENCE** Worldwide in igneous and metamorphic rocks, or as waterworn pebbles in alluvial deposits. The finest stones come from Burma; those from Thailand, the main source, are brownish red; Afghanistan, Pakistan, and Vietnam produce bright red stones; those from India, North Carolina (USA), Russia, Australia, and Norway are dark, sometimes even opaque.

*• mixed-cut is typical for rubies*

*star effect seen in cabochons when rutile • inclusions present*

**CUSHION MIXED-CUT**

• **REMARK** In 1902, a Frenchman, Auguste Verneuil, produced a synthetic ruby crystal by exposing powdered aluminium oxide and colouring material to the flame of a blowtorch.

*manufactured by • Verneuil method*

Colour zoning indicates the layers of growth in a crystal. They can be seen here as a series of concentric hexagons, which appear parallel to the prismatic crystal faces.

*stone • weighs over 138 carats*

**ROSSER REEVES RUBY**

**STEP-CUT SYNTHETIC**

*pinkish red crystal •*

*purplish • red coloration*

**CABOCHON**

*largest gem-quality crystals are from Burma •*

Brilliant  Step  Cabochon  Mixed

**BURMESE RUBY CRYSTAL**

| SG 4.00 | RI 1.76–1.77 | DR 0.008 | Lustre Vitreous |
|---|---|---|---|

| Crystal structure Trigonal | Composition Aluminium oxide | Hardness 9 |
|---|---|---|

# SAPPHIRE (CORUNDUM)

All gem-quality corundum that is not red is called sapphire, yet this name is popularly associated with the colour blue. Variation in colour, due to iron and titanium impurities, spans many shades, but the most valuable is a clear, deep blue. Some stones, called "colour-change sapphire", exhibit different shades of blue in artificial and natural light.

• OCCURRENCE Good quality sapphire is found in Burma, Sri Lanka, and India. The best Indian sapphire is cornflower blue, and found in Kashmir, either in pegmatites or as waterworn pebbles in alluvial deposits. Sapphire from Thailand, Australia, and Nigeria is dark blue, and may appear nearly black. Montana (USA) produces sapphire of an attractive metallic blue. Other localities include Cambodia, Brazil, Kenya, Malawi, and Colombia.

• REMARK Synthetic sapphire production began in the late 19th century. Commercial quantities became available in the early 20th century.

• rutile inclusions create 6-rayed star effect in cabochons

STAR CABOCHON

pale blue Sri
• Lankan stone

CARVED BUDDHA
Since the Middle Ages, sapphire has symbolized the tranquillity of the heavens, bestowing peace and amiability upon the wearer, and suppressing wicked and impure thoughts.

BRILLIANT-CUT

"Kashmir blue"
• crystals

Brilliant    Cabochon    Cameo

sapphire crystal •
has intergrown
with tourmaline

BLUE SAPPHIRE
CRYSTAL

• black
tourmaline

| SG 4.00 | RI 1.76–1.77 | DR 0.008 | Lustre Vitreous |
|---|---|---|---|

| Crystal structure Trigonal | Composition Aluminium oxide | Hardness 9 |
|---|---|---|

# PADPARADSCHA (CORUNDUM)

Padparadscha is a very rare, pinkish orange sapphire. It is the only variety of corundum other than ruby that is given its own name, rather than being referred to as a sapphire of a particular colour. The name derives from a Sinhalese word, meaning lotus blossom.

• OCCURRENCE Sri Lanka.

• REMARK Like all varieties of corundum, padparadscha is an excellent jewellery stone, as it is second only to diamond in hardness.

characteristic
pinkish orange
• colour

vitreous
lustre •

• truncated
heart shape

Mixed

MIXED-CUT

| SG 4.00 | RI 1.76–1.77 | DR 0.008 | Lustre Vitreous |
|---|---|---|---|

| Crystal structure Trigonal | Composition Aluminium oxide | Hardness 9 |
|---|---|---|

# COLOURLESS SAPPHIRE (CORUNDUM)

The different colours found within members of the corundum group are due to small amounts of metal oxide impurities. Corundum without impurities (and therefore without colour) is rare, but when found is classified as colourless sapphire. Stones made up of different colours, including colourless areas, are more common. Stones like these are generally orientated by the cutter so that the colour is at the base. Then, when viewed from above, colour fills the stone.

• OCCURRENCE Truly colourless sapphire is found in Sri Lanka. Cloudy or milky coloured sapphire is also found in Sri Lanka, and referred to locally as *geuda*. Heat treatment of *geuda* produces blue sapphire, much of which is faceted and used in jewellery. Some Sri Lankan corundum shows red, blue, and colourless areas, which may be faceted or polished to give an interesting stone.

• REMARK Synthetic colourless corundum has been produced by the Verneuil method since about the 1920s, and has been called diamondite.

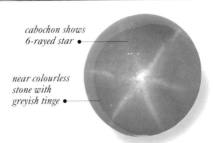

cabochon shows 6-rayed star •

near colourless stone with greyish tinge •

**STAR-STONE CABOCHON**

elongated cut •

• colourless sapphire is free from impurities

**OVAL MIXED-CUT**

bubble-like inclusions •

pyramidal end •

• pure, colourless stones are rare

twinned, • prismatic crystal

**MIXED-CUT**

**COLOURLESS CRYSTAL**

Brilliant    Brilliant    Cabochon

| SG 4.00 | RI 1.76–1.77 | DR 0.008 | Lustre Vitreous |
|---|---|---|---|

| Crystal structure Trigonal | Composition Aluminium oxide | Hardness 9 |
|---|---|---|

# GREEN SAPPHIRE (CORUNDUM)

From medieval times until the end of the 19th century green sapphire was referred to as "oriental peridot". Many sapphires that appear green actually consist of very fine alternating bands of blue and yellow sapphire, which may be visible under a microscope.

• OCCURRENCE Green sapphires are found in Thailand, Sri Lanka, and Australia (Queensland and New South Wales).

Brilliant

very dark • green colour

• vitreous lustre

**CUSHION-CUT**

| SG 4.00 | RI 1.76–1.77 | DR 0.008 | Lustre Vitreous |
|---|---|---|---|

| Crystal structure Trigonal | Composition Aluminium oxide | Hardness 9 |
|---|---|---|

# PINK SAPPHIRE (CORUNDUM)

Pure pink sapphire is coloured by very small quantities of chromium, and with increasing amounts of chromium it forms a continuous colour range with ruby. Tiny amounts of iron may produce pink-orange stones called padparadscha (see p.95), or iron and titanium impurities together may make a purplish stone. Pink sapphires are often cut with a deep profile.
• **OCCURRENCE** Pink sapphires, from a very pale and delicate pink to a near-red, occur in Sri Lanka, Burma, and East Africa.
• **REMARK** Like rubies (see p.94), pink sapphires are believed to ward off ill-health and misfortune. For the wearer to gain the benefit of the stone, however, it is thought necessary for it to be worn directly on the skin. Therefore stones are cut so that, when set in a piece of jewellery, the back makes contact with the skin.

*• pink colour derives from chromium*

*• Sri Lankan stones range from pale pink to red*

**CUSHION MIXED-CUT**

*stones may be worn next to the • skin for maximum benefit*

**OVAL MIXED-CUT**

*striations on • crystal face*

**PINK SAPPHIRE CRYSTAL**

Brilliant    Cushion    Pendeloque

| SG 4.00 | RI 1.76–1.77 | DR 0.008 | Lustre Vitreous |
|---|---|---|---|

| Crystal structure Trigonal | Composition Aluminium oxide | Hardness 9 |
|---|---|---|

# YELLOW SAPPHIRE (CORUNDUM)

Up until the end of the 19th century yellow sapphire was known as "oriental topaz" (only blue corundum was called sapphire). Nevertheless yellow and greenish yellow sapphires make unusual and attractive gemstones in their own right.
• **OCCURRENCE** In Queensland and New South Wales (Australia), a greenish yellow sapphire is found that may be faceted. Similar stones occur in Thailand, and purely yellow stones in Sri Lanka, Montana (USA), and East Africa.

*• yellow sapphire formerly known as oriental topaz*

*barrel-shaped crystal with • tapering ends*

**CUSHION MIXED-CUT**

Brilliant

**WATERWORN CRYSTAL**

| SG 4.00 | RI 1.76–1.77 | DR 0.008 | Lustre Vitreous |
|---|---|---|---|

| Crystal structure Trigonal | Composition Calcium carbonate | Hardness 3 |
|---|---|---|

# CALCITE

Common worldwide, calcite is the principal component of limestones and marbles, and of most stalactites and stalagmites. It can also be found as large, transparent, colourless, complex crystals, or as prismatic crystals intergrown with other minerals. Because of its softness it is only faceted for the collector, but marbles and brown, banded calcite from limestone caves are both used for decoration and carving.

• calcite crystals are highly birefringent

• vitreous lustre on front, pearly lustre at sides

red tinge due to iron oxides •

• **OCCURRENCE** Italy is famous for fine quality marbles, particularly the creamy Carrara marble. Transparent, colourless rhombs are known as "Iceland spar"; a white fibrous variety, cut *en cabochon*, shows the cat's-eye effect. Pink and green crystals occur in the USA, Germany, and England.

"ICELAND SPAR" RHOMB

*transparent, colourless crystals •*

Step    Polished

PRISMATIC CALCITE CRYSTALS

| SG 2.71 | RI 1.48–1.66 | DR 0.172 | Lustre Vitreous to pearly |
|---|---|---|---|

| Crystal structure Trigonal | Composition Beryllium silicate | Hardness 7½ |
|---|---|---|

# PHENAKITE

Phenakite is a rare mineral, found as white or colourless tabular crystals or stubby prisms. Twinning is common and distinguishes it from rock crystal (see p.81), with which it is often confused (hence its name, derived from the Greek word for cheat). Transparent crystals are faceted for the collector, and are hard and bright.

• phenakite has silvery look when cut well

• vitreous lustre

BRILLIANT-CUT

• **OCCURRENCE** Phenakite occurs in pegmatites, granites, and mica schists. The best crystals are found in the Urals (Russia), Brazil, and Colorado (USA). Other localities include Italy, Sri Lanka, Zimbabwe, and Namibia.

*only transparent stones are faceted*

crystals have wedge-shaped ends •

• **REMARK** A pebble weighing 1,470 carats was found in Sri Lanka, and faceted to a 569-carat oval and several smaller stones.

Brilliant    Mixed

BRILLIANT-CUT

PHENAKITE CRYSTAL

| SG 2.96 | RI 1.65–1.67 | DR 0.015 | Lustre Vitreous |
|---|---|---|---|

| Crystal structure Trigonal | Composition Hydrated copper silicate | Hardness 5 |
|---|---|---|

# DIOPTASE

Dioptase is a beautiful, vivid emerald-green, with a hint of blue. It has very high fire, but this is masked by its strong colour, which may make stones translucent rather than transparent. Prized by the collector for its colour, it is nonetheless rarely faceted, as stones are brittle and fragile, and too soft to be worn. It is sometimes confused with emerald.
• OCCURRENCE The best quality crystals are found in copper deposits in Russia, Namibia, Zaire, Chile, and Arizona (USA).

*crystals have perfect cleavage*

*emerald- to bluish green coloration*

**DIOPTASE CRYSTALS**

Brilliant

Cabochon

| SG 3.31 | RI 1.67–1.72 | DR 0.053 | Lustre Vitreous |
|---|---|---|---|

| Crystal structure Trigonal | Composition Magnesium and calcium carbonate | Hardness 3½ |
|---|---|---|

# DOLOMITE

Dolomite is found as colourless, white, pink, or yellow crystals, often with distinctive curved faces. Rarely faceted, because of its softness and perfect cleavage, its main use is in massive form, as a decorative stone.
• OCCURRENCE Found in limestones and marbles, the best crystals are from Italy, Switzerland, Germany, and the USA.

*curved faces*

**TWIN CRYSTAL**

*colourless quartz*

*opaque, dolomite crystals*

**TWINNED DOLOMITE CRYSTALS IN MATRIX**

Step    Step

| SG 2.85 | RI 1.50–1.68 | DR 0.179 | Lustre Vitreous to Pearly |
|---|---|---|---|

| Crystal structure Trigonal | Composition Zinc carbonate | Hardness 5 |
|---|---|---|

# SMITHSONITE

Smithsonite is usually found as bluish green or green botryoidal masses or soft layers, which are polished and used as an ornamental stone (sometimes called bonamite). It may also be coloured pink by cobalt, or yellow by cadmium. Crystals may also be found, but are faceted for the collector only.
• OCCURRENCE Colourless crystals in Namibia and Zambia; blue-green masses in the USA, Spain, and Greece; yellow in the USA and Sardinia.

*blue smithsonite crust*

*opaque, white smithsonite*

**SMITHSONITE ON MATRIX**

**SMITHSONITE ON MATRIX**

Cabochon

*pearly lustre*

| SG 4.35 | RI 1.62–1.85 | DR 0.230 | Lustre Pearly |
|---|---|---|---|

| Crystal structure Trigonal | Composition Manganese carbonate | Hardness 4 |
|---|---|---|

# RHODOCHROSITE

Rhodochrosite derives its pink colour from manganese. Gem-quality crystals do occur, and are cut for collectors, but the fine-grained, banded rock is more commonly used for decoration.
• OCCURRENCE Rhodochrosite occurs in veins associated with manganese, copper, silver, and lead deposits. Argentina has the oldest mines, and banded rhodochrosite from there is sometimes called "Inca rose". Today, the prime commercial sources are in the USA.

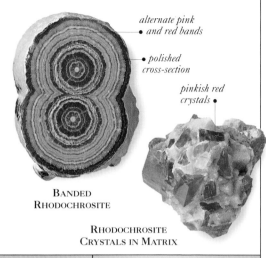

*alternate pink
• and red bands*

*• polished
cross-section*

*pinkish red
crystals •*

BANDED
RHODOCHROSITE

RHODOCHROSITE
CRYSTALS IN MATRIX

Bead        Cabochon        Cameo

| SG 3.60 | RI 1.60–1.80 | DR 0.220 | Lustre Vitreous to pearly |
|---|---|---|---|

| Crystal structure Trigonal | Composition Iron oxide | Hardness 6½ |
|---|---|---|

# HEMATITE

Hematite usually occurs as massive, opaque material with a metallic lustre, showing a blood-red colour when cut into thin slices. However, it can also occur as short, black, rhombohedral crystals, and may have iridescent surfaces. When arranged like the petals of a flower, hematite is called an "iron rose". Shiny crystals may be called "specular" hematite, a name derived from their traditional use in mirrors.
• OCCURRENCE Main deposits are in igneous rocks in North America (Lake Superior and Quebec), Brazil, Venezuela, and England. Iron roses are found in Switzerland and Brazil; cuttable material in England, Germany, and Elba.
• REMARK Powdered, it may be used as an artist's pigment or for polishing. In the past it was used to protect the wearer from bleeding.

CARVED FROG
With a hardness of 6½, hematite is easily carved, but care must be taken to prevent scratching. This oriental-style frog has a grey metallic lustre.

*shiny crystals
were once used
• as mirrors*

*play of light
• on surface*

"SPECULAR" HEMATITE

*"iron rose" •
arrangement
of crystals*

IRIDESCENT
HEMATITE CRYSTALS

Bead        Cabochon        Cameo

| SG 5.20 | RI 2.94–3.22 | DR 0.280 | Lustre Metallic |
|---|---|---|---|

| Crystal structure Trigonal | Composition Complex borosilicate | | Hardness 7½ |
|---|---|---|---|

# RUBELLITE (TOURMALINE)

Members of the tourmaline family of minerals have the same basic crystal structure, but occur in many colours. Rubellite (from the Latin for red) is the name given to the pink or red variety, with ruby-red stones the most highly prized. Rubellite crystals are striated, with a triangular cross-section and a rounded outline. They may also occur with a fibrous habit, and show a cat's-eye when cut *en cabochon*.
• OCCURRENCE Russian pink and red tourmaline occurs in weathered granites. Other sites include Madagascar, the USA, Brazil, Burma, and East Africa.
• REMARK The specific gravity of tourmaline varies with colour – dark red has a higher SG than pink.

*dark pink colour*

*fibrous habit visible in cat's-eye "flash"*

CABOCHON

*translucent stone*

*rubellite crystals*

*rock crystal*

RECTANGULAR STEP-CUT

RUBELLITE CRYSTALS IN MATRIX

Pendeloque

Step

Cabochon

| SG 3.06 | RI 1.62–1.64 | DR 0.018 | Lustre Vitreous |
|---|---|---|---|

| Crystal structure Trigonal | Composition Complex borosilicate | | Hardness 7½ |
|---|---|---|---|

# INDICOLITE (TOURMALINE)

Dark blue tourmaline is called indicolite or, occasionally, indigolite. Indicolite is often heat-treated to lighten its colour and produce a more attractive stone.
• OCCURRENCE An important source for indicolite is Siberia (Russia), where it occurs in yellow clays formed from weathered granites. Fine, bright blue tourmaline has recently been found in Paraiba, Brazil. Other localities include Madagascar and the USA.
• REMARK A lilac to violet-blue or reddish blue variety (first found in Russia) is known as siberite.

*inky-blue, semi-translucent stone*

*greenish blue, transparent stone from Brazil*

OVAL MIXED-CUT

*fractured surface*

*vertical striations*

RECTANGULAR STEP-CUT

INDICOLITE CRYSTAL

Step

Step

| SG 3.06 | RI 1.62–1.64 | DR 0.018 | Lustre Vitreous |
|---|---|---|---|

| Crystal structure Trigonal | Composition Complex borosilicate | Hardness 7½ |
|---|---|---|

# DRAVITE (TOURMALINE)

Dravite is a very dark coloured (usually brown) form of tourmaline, rich in magnesium. It is possible to lighten the colour by heat treatment. Dravite shows strong dichroism, and should therefore be cut with the table facet parallel to the length of the crystal in order to show a lighter and more attractive colour.

• OCCURRENCE Dravite can occur as single crystals, or as parallel or radiating groups. Brown tourmaline and yellow tourmaline occur together in the gem gravels of Sri Lanka. It is also found in the USA, Canada, Mexico, Brazil, and Australia.

• REMARK The name "dravite" is derived from the district of Drave, in Austria.

*golden brown colour*

*stones may be lightened by heat treatment*

ROUND BRILLIANT-CUT

*orange-brown colour*

CUSHION MIXED-CUT

*prismatic habit*

*opaque, dark brown crystal*

CRYSTAL FRAGMENT

Brilliant

Brilliant

Cushion

| SG 3.06 | RI 1.61–1.63 | DR 0.018 | Lustre Vitreous |
|---|---|---|---|

| Crystal structure Trigonal | Composition Complex borosilicate | Hardness 7½ |
|---|---|---|

# ACHROITE (TOURMALINE)

This particularly rare, colourless stone is a variety of elbaite, a member of the tourmaline group. It does not show the strong dichroism characteristic of most tourmaline varieties and therefore can be cut with the table facet either parallel or perpendicular to the length of the crystal. Colourless tourmaline may also be produced by applying heat to light pink tourmalines.

• OCCURRENCE Achroite occurs with coloured tourmalines in the pegmatites of Madagascar and Pala (in California in the USA).

• REMARK Achroite is named after the Greek word *achroos*, meaning "without colour".

*transparent, colourless stone*

*girdle around "waist" of stone*

ROUND BRILLIANT-CUT

*fracture is conchoidal*

OVAL BRILLIANT-CUT

ACHROITE CRYSTAL

Brilliant

Brilliant

Mixed

| SG 3.06 | RI 1.62–1.64 | DR 0.018 | Lustre Vitreous |
|---|---|---|---|

| Crystal structure Trigonal | Composition Complex borosilicate | Hardness 7½ |
|---|---|---|

# WATERMELON TOURMALINE

Tourmaline crystals with a pink centre and a green rim, or vice-versa, are called watermelon tourmaline, because their colouring is similar to the pink flesh and green rind of a watermelon. Many other tourmalines are made up of two or more colours, individual crystals containing up to 15 different colours or shades.

• **OCCURRENCE** Watermelon tourmaline is found in South Africa, East Africa, Brazil, and in many other localities.

• **REMARK** Parti- and multicoloured tourmaline is carved or cut and polished to show off the different colours to best effect.

Baguette

Cabochon

*green and pink parts occur in single crystal*

*characteristic colour zoning*

TABLE-CUT

CRYSTAL SECTION

| SG 3.06 | RI 1.62–1.64 | DR 0.018 | Lustre Vitreous |
|---|---|---|---|

| Crystal structure Trigonal | Composition Complex borosilicate | Hardness 7½ |
|---|---|---|

# SCHORL (TOURMALINE)

Schorl is the black, iron-rich form of tourmaline, and is very common. The opaque, prismatic crystals may be several metres in length.

• **OCCURRENCE** Found in pegmatites.

• **REMARK** During the Victorian era, black tourmaline was widely used for mourning jewellery, but today it has little, if any, value as a gemstone.

Brilliant

Mixed

*broken, worn end*

*vertical striations*

SCHORL CRYSTAL

| SG 3.06 | RI 1.62–1.67 | DR 0.018 | Lustre Vitreous |
|---|---|---|---|

| Crystal structure Trigonal | Composition Complex borosilicate | Hardness 7½ |
|---|---|---|

# GREEN AND YELLOW TOURMALINE

Yellow-green is the most common of all tourmaline colour varieties, but emerald-green is much rarer and more valuable. Indeed, until the 18th century it was often confused with emerald.

• **OCCURRENCE** Emerald-green stones are found in Brazil, Tanzania, and Namibia; fibrous yellow material occurs in Sri Lanka.

Brilliant

*semi-transparent stone*

*greenish yellow is most common colour variety*

BRILLIANT-CUT

| SG 3.06 | RI 1.62–1.64 | DR 0.018 | Lustre Vitreous |
|---|---|---|---|

| Crystal structure Orthorhombic | Composition Calcium carbonate | | Hardness 3½ |
|---|---|---|---|

# ARAGONITE

Aragonite is usually transparent or translucent, and colourless or white when pure. Impurities may cause shades of yellow, blue, pink, or green to occur. It is found in many different habits: small, elongate, prismatic crystals form in radiating groups, and concretions and stalactites are also common. It has poor cleavage.

• OCCURRENCE Found mainly in sedimentary environments, aragonite may form as tufa (porous rock) in Czechoslovakia and Turkey. Other localities include Spain, Colorado (USA), France, and Cumbria (England).

*layering revealed in cut and polished • section*

**STALACTITIC POLISHED SLAB**

*crystals growing • out of matrix*

*crystals colourless when pure •*

Bead

Polished

**CRYSTAL SPRAYS ON MATRIX**

| SG 2.94 | RI 1.53–1.68 | DR 0.155 | Lustre Vitreous |
|---|---|---|---|

| Crystal structure Orthorhombic | Composition Barium sulphate | | Hardness 3 |
|---|---|---|---|

# BARYTE

Baryte occurs in a variety of colours, including colourless, white, yellow, and blue, but its softness, perfect cleavage, brittleness, and high density make it of little use as a gemstone, and it is cut for collectors only. Crystals vary a great deal and may be transparent to opaque, with a variety of habits from tabular to massive.

• OCCURRENCE Baryte is commonly found in lead and silver mines. It also occurs in limestones, and may be deposited by hot springs. Crystals up to 1m (40in) in length have been found in Cumbria, Cornwall, and Derbyshire, in England. Other good localities include Czechoslovakia, Romania, Germany, the USA, and Italy.

*stones are faceted for collectors • only*

**OCTAGONAL MIXED-CUT**

*tabular, double-ended • crystal*

*crystal layers build in concentric bands as stalagmite • forms*

*stones are • easily damaged*

**STALAGMITE SECTION**

*growth zones •*

**BARYTE CRYSTAL**

Step

Mixed

Polished

| SG 4.45 | RI 1.63–1.65 | DR 0.012 | Lustre Vitreous to pearly |
|---|---|---|---|

| Crystal structure Orthorhombic | Composition Strontium sulphate | | Hardness 3½ |
|---|---|---|---|

# CELESTINE

Celestine is usually found as colourless, milky white, yellow, orange, or pale blue prismatic crystals, or in fine-grained masses. With a hardness of only 3½ on Mohs' scale and perfect cleavage, celestine is extremely fragile. It has been cut for the collector, however, and some fine specimens can be seen in museums.
• OCCURRENCE Celestine may occur with sandstones or limestones, in evaporite deposits, in pegmatites, in cavities in volcanic rocks, or with galena and sphalerite in mineral veins. Most of the material that is capable of being faceted is found in either Namibia or Madagascar. It is also found in Italy (including Sicily), England, Czechoslovakia, the USA, and Canada.

*colourless celestine is the most common*
• *variety*

*cut stones are rare and*
• *lack fire*

MIXED-CUT

*transparent to semi-translucent colourless*
• *crystal*

*sulphur matrix* •

*colourless celestine crystals* •

Brilliant    Mixed    CELESTINE CRYSTAL

CRYSTALS IN MATRIX

| SG 3.98 | RI 1.62–1.63 | DR 0.010 | Lustre Vitreous to pearly |
|---|---|---|---|

| Crystal structure Orthorhombic | Composition Lead carbonate | | Hardness 3½ |
|---|---|---|---|

# CERUSSITE

Cerussite is usually colourless, but white, grey, and black specimens have been found. Its two most distinctive features are its high density and its adamantine lustre. Crystals have a stubby tabular or elongate habit. Although attractive, it is too soft to have much value as a gemstone, and is cut solely for collectors.
• OCCURRENCE Cerussite is usually found around lead ores. Large, clear, transparent, colourless, cuttable crystals have been found in Tsumeb (Namibia). Other localities include Austria, Australia, Czechoslovakia, the USA, Germany, Scotland, and Italy, including Sardinia.
• REMARK Sometimes confused with diamond and other colourless gems, it may be distinguished by its higher density.

• *very pale grey colour*

*worn facet edges*
• *due to softness*

ROUND BRILLIANT-CUT

*colourless, crystal "twin"* •

Brilliant    Brilliant

*surface formerly* •
*attached to matrix*

PRISMATIC CRYSTAL

| SG 6.51 | RI 1.80–2.08 | DR 0.274 | Lustre Adamantine |
|---|---|---|---|

| Crystal structure Orthorhombic | Composition Aluminium fluorohydroxysilicate | Hardness 8 |
|---|---|---|

# TOPAZ

Topaz occurs in a range of different colours: deep golden yellow topaz (sometimes called sherry topaz) and pink topaz are the most valuable; blue and green stones are also popular. Natural pink stones are rare – most pink topaz is heat-treated yellow material. Much colourless topaz is irradiated and heat-treated to a range of blues, some almost indistinguishable from aquamarine when seen with the naked eye. Some topaz has tear-shaped cavities, containing a gas bubble or several immiscible (non-mixing) liquids. Other inclusions such as cracks, streaks, and veils also occur. Prismatic topaz crystals have a characteristic lozenge-shaped cross-section and striations parallel to their length. Topaz has one perfect cleavage.

• OCCURRENCE Topaz occurs in igneous rocks such as pegmatites, granites, and volcanic lavas. It may also be found in alluvial deposits as waterworn pebbles. Localities include Brazil, the USA, Sri Lanka, Burma, the former USSR, Australia, Tasmania, Pakistan, Mexico, Japan, and Africa. Brazil, Pakistan, and Russia are sources of pink topaz.

• REMARK In the 17th century the Braganza diamond (1,640 carats) in the Portuguese crown was thought to be the largest diamond ever found. This was never confirmed and it is now believed to have been a colourless topaz. The name "topaz" is thought to be derived from the Sanskrit word *tapas*, meaning fire.

*pale yellow* • *topaz*

• *stones up to 35,000 carats have been faceted*

OVAL MIXED-CUT

*pink colour* • *variety*

• *set in gold and worn around the neck, topaz is reputed to dispel bad omens, heal poor vision, and calm anger*

OVAL STEP-CUT

*characteristic wedge-shaped* • *ends*

TOPAZ RING
A salmon-pink, step-cut, eight-sided topaz, set in a gold ring.

FLOWER BROOCH
The heart of this flower-shaped brooch is a round brilliant-cut topaz, surrounded by 36 sherry-coloured topaz gems – some triangular, some diamond-shaped.

TRANSPARENT, SHERRY-COLOURED CRYSTAL

| SG 3.54 | RI 1.62–1.63 | DR 0.010 | Lustre Vitreous |
|---|---|---|---|

very pale
greyish green
colour •

stones are
typically
• transparent

• 21,005-
carat
stone, once
the largest
gem ever
faceted

**SQUARE CUSHION-CUT
("THE BRAZILIAN PRINCESS")**

**ELONGATED OVAL MIXED-CUT**

blue topaz is
• also popular

pale green
topaz crystal •

• blue topaz
may be
produced by
heat-treating
colourless
stones

**TOPAZ CRYSTAL
IN MATRIX**

• pegmatite
rock

**OCTAGONAL STEP-CUT**

stone is partially
cut, before being
heat-treated to
• turn it blue

characteristic
tear-shaped
inclusions •

Brilliant

Cushion

Pendeloque

Step

Step

Mixed

**PENDELOQUE CUT**

**COLOURLESS, PARTIALLY
FACETED PEBBLE**

| Crystal structure Orthorhombic | Composition Beryllium aluminium oxide | Hardness 8½ |
|---|---|---|

# CHRYSOBERYL

Chrysoberyl occurs in a range of colours, from green, greenish yellow, and yellow, to brown. It is a hard, durable stone, particularly suitable for use in jewellery. When cut well, gems are brilliant but lack fire. Two varieties, alexandrite and cat's-eye, have unique qualities of their own. The very rare and valuable alexandrite changes from green in daylight to red, mauve, or brown under incandescent light, such as a light bulb. Synthetic chrysoberyl, synthetic corundum, and synthetic spinel have all been produced to imitate alexandrite's colour change. Cat's-eye, when cut *en cabochon*, has a near-white line across a yellowish grey stone, due to canal- or feather-like fluid inclusions, or needle-like inclusions of rutile. The most highly prized cat's-eye colour is a light golden brown, often with a shadow that gives a light and dark, "milk and honey" effect. Pale yellow chrysoberyl, popular in 18th- and 19th-century Portuguese jewellery, was also known as chrysolite.

• OCCURRENCE Although mainly worked out, the best chrysoberyl, including alexandrite, has been found in mica schists in the Urals (Russia). The largest faceted chrysoberyl from Russia weighs 66 carats. Large waterworn pebbles of various colours are found in the gem gravels of Sri Lanka. Chrysoberyl also occurs in Burma, Brazil, Zimbabwe, Tanzania, and Madagascar. Cat's-eye is found in Sri Lanka, Brazil, and China.

• REMARK The name is from the Greek *chrysos*, meaning golden, and *beryllos*, which refers to the beryllium content. Known for thousands of years in Asia, it was highly valued for the protection it afforded from the "evil eye".

*transparent stone*

*dark greenish brown colour*

**CUSHION MIXED-CUT**

*golden brown colour is highly prized*

*cut stones are brilliant, but may lack fire*

**CUSHION MIXED-CUT**

*greenish yellow cabochon shows faint cat's-eye*

*cat's-eye chrysoberyl has also been known as cymophane*

**POLISHED CABOCHON**

**FINGER RING**
This ring, made of many cushion-cut chrysoberyl stones in a gold setting, is probably of 18th-century Spanish origin. The chrysoberyl was collected from a vein running through chalk.

*greenish yellow twinned crystals*

*typical wedge-shaped ends*

**SPRAY OF CHRYSOBERYL CRYSTALS**

| SG 3.71 | RI 1.74–1.75 | DR 0.009 | Lustre Vitreous |
|---|---|---|---|

alexandrite
stones show a
colour change in
• incandescent light

alexandrite was found on the
birthday of Tsar Alexander II,
and named after him •

• golden
brown
changes
to red

**ALEXANDRITE MIXED-CUT**

**ALEXANDRITE CRYSTALS**

• intergrown
crystals

only chrysoberyl cat's-
eye may be termed
simply "cat's-eye" •

cloudy blue
flash in
cat's-eye •

dark brown
stone with
orange and
• red tinges

• cat's-
eye
effect

**CAT'S-EYE DOUBLE
CABOCHON**

**CAT'S-EYE CABOCHON**

minute, tube-like
inclusions produce
chatoyancy •

**CAT'S-EYE DOUBLE
CABOCHON**

**CHRYSOBERYL CROSS**
A cross made up of eleven
specimens of yellow-green
chrysoberyl, each cut as a
double cabochon to show
the cat's-eye effect. The
stones are arranged so that
the flash across the centre
of each cabochon is in a
variety of positions.

Brilliant    Cushion

Cabochon    Mixed

**VICTORIAN BROOCH**
This exquisite brooch
from the Victorian era in
Britain is made up of
greenish yellow, faceted
chrysoberyls set in gold
filigree. Its hardness and
durability make chryso-
beryl a particularly good
stone for use in jewellery.

| Crystal structure Orthorhombic | Composition Aluminium silicate | | Hardness 7½ |
|---|---|---|---|

# ANDALUSITE

Andalusite varies in colour from a pale yellowish brown to a dark bottle-green, dark brown, or the most popular greenish red. It has very strong and distinctive pleochroism, so that, when turned, the same stone may appear yellow, green, and red. Large crystals may be vertically striated prisms with a square cross-section and pyramidal ends, but are rare. More usual are opaque, rod-like aggregates of crystals or waterworn pebbles. It is the pebbles that are usually cut as gemstones.

• **OCCURRENCE** Andalusite is usually found in pegmatites. Pebbles occur in the gem gravels of Sri Lanka and Brazil. Other localities include Spain, Canada, Russia, Australia, and the USA.

• **REMARK** An opaque, yellowish grey variety, chiastolite, occurs as long prisms, which make a cross when cut and polished.

*• pleochroism creates flashes of yellow, green, and red*

**OCTAGONAL STEP-CUT**

*"cross" once used as religious • symbol*

*opaque crystals with rhombic • cross-section*

*• cut and polished surface*

**CHIASTOLITE CROSS-SECTION**

**ANDALUSITE CRYSTALS IN MATRIX**

Brilliant

Baguette

| SG 3.16 | RI 1.63–1.64 | DR 0.010 | Lustre Vitreous |
|---|---|---|---|

| Crystal structure Orthorhombic | Composition Calcium borosilicate | | Hardness 7 |
|---|---|---|---|

# DANBURITE

Generally colourless, danburite crystals may also be yellow or pink. They form wedge-shaped prisms, similar to those of colourless topaz but distinguishable by cleavage (poor in danburite, perfect in topaz) and specific gravity (lower in danburite).

• **OCCURRENCE** First found in the town of Danbury, Connecticut (USA). Gem-quality crystals occur in Burma, Mexico, Switzerland, Italy, and Japan.

*Burmese stone with slight yellowish tinge •*

*stones are bright but • lack fire*

*characteristic wedge-shaped • end*

**BRILLIANT-CUT**

**WHITE DANBURITE CRYSTALS**

Brilliant

Step

Mixed

| SG 3.00 | RI 1.63–1.64 | DR 0.006 | Lustre Vitreous to greasy |
|---|---|---|---|

| Crystal structure Orthorhombic | Composition Magnesium iron silicate | Hardness 5½ |
|---|---|---|

# ENSTATITE

Enstatite is one of the pyroxene family – a series of magnesium- to iron-rich silicates. Crystals occur as short prisms, but are rare: most gem-quality material is faceted from rolled pebbles. Cuttable enstatite varies in colour from a grey- to yellowish green or olive-green, to an iron-rich brownish green. A brilliant emerald-green variety, coloured by chromium, also occurs.

• OCCURRENCE Enstatite is often found with kimberlites in South Africa. Brownish green enstatite is found in Burma, Norway, and California (USA). Some Sri Lankan and Indian enstatite is chatoyant. It also occurs in the USA, Switzerland, Greenland, Scotland, Japan, and the former USSR.

*double cabochon-cut shows cat's-eye effect •*

CAT'S-EYE CABOCHON

*• clear, yellowish green stone from South Africa*

OVAL MIXED-CUT

*uneven fracture •*

*massive, fibrous material •*

Step

Cabochon

ENSTATITE ROUGH

| SG 3.27 | RI 1.66–1.67 | DR 0.010 | Lustre Vitreous |
|---|---|---|---|

| Crystal structure Orthorhombic | Composition Aluminium silicate | Hardness 7½ |
|---|---|---|

# SILLIMANITE

Sillimanite (named after Professor Silliman of Yale University, USA) is blue to green, with distinct pleochroism showing pale yellowish green, dark green, and blue from different angles. When crystals occur in long slender prisms in parallel groups, resembling fibres, the material is often called fibrolite.

• OCCURRENCE Sillimanite is found in metamorphic rocks and occasionally in pegmatites. Blue and violet stones are found in Burma; greenish grey stones in Sri Lanka; fibrolite in Idaho (USA). Other sites include Czechoslovakia, India, Italy, Germany, and Brazil.

*• pale violet stone from Burma*

*• scissors-cut crown facets*

CUSHION MIXED-CUT

*perpendicular fibres •*

*long, slender • crystals*

FIBROLITE CABOCHON

SILLIMANITE CRYSTALS IN MATRIX

Cushion

Cabochon

| SG 3.25 | RI 1.66–1.68 | DR 0.019 | Lustre Vitreous |
|---|---|---|---|

| Crystal structure Orthorhombic | Composition Iron magnesium silicate | Hardness 5½ |
|---|---|---|

# HYPERSTHENE

Hypersthene is an iron-rich pyroxene in the same series of minerals as enstatite (see p.111) and bronzite. It is distinguished by its reddish iridescence, which is due to platy inclusions of goethite and hematite. Often too dark to facet, it may be cut *en cabochon* instead to show the sparkling inclusions. Bronzite, a greenish brown variety with a bronze-like lustre, is also a collector's stone – dark, slightly brittle, and not generally used in jewellery.

• OCCURRENCE Most gem hypersthene is found in India, Norway, Greenland, Germany, and the USA. Bronzite is found in Austria.

*colours range from green to greyish black and brown*

**RECTANGULAR STEP-CUT**

*opaque crystal fragment*

*brassy effect*

*platy inclusions visible*

**POLISHED BRONZITE**

**HYPERSTHENE ROUGH**

Cushion    Baguette

| SG 3.35 | RI 1.65–1.67 | DR 0.010 | Lustre Vitreous |
|---|---|---|---|

| Crystal structure Orthorhombic | Composition Magnesium aluminium silicate | Hardness 7 |
|---|---|---|

# IOLITE

Violet-blue iolite (also known as cordierite) has been called water sapphire because of its similarity to blue sapphire when cut. It can be recognized by its strong pleochroism, visible without equipment, which gives the gem its other name of dichroite. The best blue colour is seen down the length of prismatic crystals; they may appear colourless when viewed across.

• OCCURRENCE Gem-quality iolite is found in alluvial deposits as small, transparent, waterworn pebbles in Sri Lanka, Burma, Madagascar, and India. Other localities include Namibia and Tanzania. Crystals are found in Germany, Norway, and Finland.

*rich violet-blue tinge*

*more intense colour visible from front*

*paler colour visible from this angle*

**IOLITE CUBE – VIEW 1**

*purplish blue crystal*

**IOLITE CUBE – VIEW 2**

Step    Cabochon    Mixed

**CRYSTAL IN MATRIX**

| SG 2.63 | RI 1.53–1.55 | DR 0.010 | Lustre Vitreous |
|---|---|---|---|

| Crystal structure Orthorhombic | Composition Magnesium aluminium borosilicate | Hardness 6½ |
|---|---|---|

# KORNERUPINE

Although kornerupine was named in 1884, it was not until 1912 that gem-quality material was found. Even now it is uncommon and cut only for collectors. Strongly pleochroic, it appears green or reddish brown when viewed from different directions. To show the best colour, it is cut with the table facet parallel to the length of the crystal.
• OCCURRENCE Localities include Madagascar, Sri Lanka, and East Africa, which also produces an emerald-green variety. Cat's-eye gems are cut from Sri Lankan and East African stones.
• REMARK It has been confused with tourmaline and enstatite.

*distinctive greyish green colour •*

RECTANGULAR STEP-CUT

MIXED-CUT

*• kornerupine gems are rare and prized by collectors*

*dark kornerupine • crystals*

CRYSTALS IN MATRIX

Cushion

Baguette

Step

| SG 3.32 | RI 1.66–1.68 | DR 0.013 | Lustre Vitreous |
|---|---|---|---|

| Crystal structure Orthorhombic | Composition Magnesium iron silicate | Hardness 6½ |
|---|---|---|

# PERIDOT

Gem-quality specimens of the mineral olivine are called peridot by gemmologists. Peridot has an olive- or bottle-green colour due to the presence of iron, and a distinctive oily or greasy lustre. It has a high birefringence, so doubling of the back facets can easily be seen in larger specimens when viewed from the front. Good-quality crystals are very rare.
• OCCURRENCE Peridot is found on St. John's Island (Egypt), in China, Burma, Brazil, Hawaii and Arizona (USA), Australia, South Africa, and Norway.
• REMARK The Crusaders brought peridot to Europe in the Middle Ages, transporting stones from St. John's Island in the Red Sea, where it had been mined for over 3,500 years.

*• green colour due to iron*

*distinctive bottle-green colour •*

OVAL MIXED-CUT

*peridot was often used in religious • jewellery*

OCTAGONAL MIXED-CUT

CRYSTAL FRAGMENT

Pendeloque

Step

Cabochon

| SG 3.34 | RI 1.64–1.69 | DR 0.036 | Lustre Vitreous to greasy |
|---|---|---|---|

| Crystal structure Orthorhombic | Composition Lead sulphate | Hardness 3 |
|---|---|---|

# ANGLESITE

Anglesite is usually colourless or with a slight yellowish tinge, but may also be found as grey, green, purple, brown, or black crystals (the black colouring is due to inclusions of galena). Crystals are heavy, but are fragile and soft, with perfect cleavage, and so are faceted for collectors only.
• OCCURRENCE Anglesite is formed by oxidation of galena (lead sulphide) and may be found in Anglesey in Wales (hence the name) and in the Leadhills district of Scotland. The best crystals are found in Tsumeb (Namibia) and Morocco. Other localities include Germany, the USA, and Sardinia.

• *stones often have a slight yellowish tinge*

*transparent anglesite crystal with pointed end* •

*galena matrix* •

FANCY-CUT

Step

ANGLESITE
CRYSTALS IN MATRIX

| SG 6.35 | RI 1.87–1.89 | DR 0.017 | Lustre Waxy to adamantine |
|---|---|---|---|

| Crystal structure Orthorhombic | Composition Magnesium aluminium iron borate | Hardness 6½ |
|---|---|---|

# SINHALITE

Until 1952, sinhalite was thought to be a brown variety of peridot, but on closer investigation it was found to be a completely new mineral. It varies from a pale yellowish brown to a dark greenish brown. Crystals have distinct pleochroism, showing pale brown, greenish brown, and dark brown when viewed from different directions. Although uncommon, sinhalite has been faceted for the collector. Cut stones may be confused with peridot, chrysoberyl, and zircon.
• OCCURRENCE Most gem-quality sinhalite is found as rolled pebbles in the gem gravels of Sri Lanka. Crystals occur in Burma but are rare. Sinhalite is also found in the former USSR, and non-gem-quality material in the USA.
• REMARK Sinhalite is named after *sinhala*, which is the Sanskrit name for Sri Lanka.

*pale yellowish brown stone* •

• *cut is slightly irregular to conserve weight*

CUSHION MIXED-CUT

*dark yellow-brown* •

CUSHION MIXED-CUT

*double-ended, waterworn prism* •

SINHALITE CRYSTAL

Step    Mixed

| SG 3.48 | RI 1.67–1.71 | DR 0.038 | Lustre Vitreous |
|---|---|---|---|

| Crystal structure Orthorhombic | Composition Beryllium hydroxyborate | Hardness 7½ |
| --- | --- | --- |

# HAMBERGITE

Hambergite, named after Axel Hamberg, the Swedish mineralogist, occurs as colourless to yellowish white crystals, but is rarely gem-quality. Brittle, with perfect cleavage, it is very fragile and suitable only for collectors. When cut, it looks like glass, but double images of the back facets may be seen through the table facet due to its high birefringence.

• OCCURRENCE Gemquality hambergite is found in Kashmir (India), and also in Madagascar.

*transparent stones for faceting are rare*

OVAL MIXED-CUT

*surface colouring from host rock*

*deep striations along length*

*brown mineral inclusions*

OVAL MIXED-CUT

HAMBERGITE
CRYSTAL

Brilliant

Step

| SG 2.35 | RI 1.55–1.63 | DR 0.072 | Lustre Vitreous |
| --- | --- | --- | --- |

| Crystal structure Orthorhombic | Composition Calcium aluminium hydroxysilicate | Hardness 6 |
| --- | --- | --- |

# PREHNITE

Often an oily green, prehnite may also range from pale yellowish to brown. Columnar or tabular crystals are rare: it occurs more usually as aggregates of barrel-shaped crystals or as botryoidal masses. Some pale yellowish brown prehnite is fibrous enough to be cut *en cabochon*, and may show the cat's-eye effect.

• OCCURRENCE Prehnite is found in basaltic volcanic rocks, intrusive igneous rocks, and in some metamorphic rocks. Pale green masses are found in Scotland; dark green or greenish brown masses in Australia; aggregates of crystals in France.

• REMARK Prehnite is named after Colonel von Prehn, who first introduced prehnite to Europe.

BRILLIANT-CUT
STONES

*stones are generally translucent*

*faceted gems are usually small*

STEP-CUT

*fractures radiate out from reddish inclusions*

*translucent crystals in botryoidal masses*

Baguette

Step

Cabochon

POLISHED FRAGMENT
CRYSTALS ON MATRIX

| SG 2.87 | RI 1.61–1.64 | DR 0.016 | Lustre Vitreous |
| --- | --- | --- | --- |

| Crystal structure Orthorhombic | Composition Calcium aluminium hydroxysilicate | Hardness 6½ |
|---|---|---|

# ZOISITE

Zoisite occurs in a number of varieties, the most sought-after being tanzanite, a variety coloured sapphire-blue by the presence of vanadium. Tanzanite crystals have distinct pleochroism, showing either purple, blue, or slate-grey depending on the angle they are viewed from. There may also be a slight colour change in incandescent light (such as that from a light bulb), when stones may appear more violet. A massive green variety of zoisite, containing rubies and occasionally dark hornblende inclusions, may be polished, carved, or tumbled to make ornaments or an attractive decorative stone. Thulite, a massive, pinkish red variety coloured by manganese, is also polished or carved to make small ornaments. Tanzanite has been confused with sapphire, and thulite with rhodonite. Some heating of zoisite varieties may enhance their colour.

• **OCCURRENCE** Tanzanite was first found in Tanzania (hence the name). Yellow and green zoisite occurs in Tanzania and Kenya. Thulite is found in Norway, Austria, western Australia, Italy, and North Carolina (USA).

• **REMARK** Discovered by Baron von Zois in the Sau-Alp mountains of Austria, zoisite was first called saualpite.

stone has been heat-treated to enhance • colour

colour varies from purple to blue due to • pleochroism

**TANZANITE MIXED-CUT**

pale bluish violet colour

stones are • soft and brittle

**TANZANITE STEP-CUT**

• tanzanite has perfect cleavage

violet-blue tanzanite • crystal

**TANZANITE CRYSTAL**

**TANZANITE CRYSTAL IN MATRIX**

• polished zoisite is often used for decorative work

**THULITE SLAB**

pinkish red colour • due to manganese

**THULITE CABOCHON**

massive habit •

intergrown greyish white quartz •

**THULITE ROUGH**

Step            Cabochon            Cameo

| SG 3.35 | RI 1.69–1.70 | DR 0.010 | Lustre Vitreous |
|---|---|---|---|

| Crystal structure Orthorhombic | Composition Aluminium iron hydroxysilicate | | Hardness 7 |
|---|---|---|---|

# STAUROLITE

Opaque, cross-shaped staurolite "twins" are used in jewellery more often than the transparent stones, which are rare and cut only for collectors. "Cross-stones", as twins are called, have been used as amulets and in religious jewellery. Crystals are reddish brown to black, with distinct pleochroism.
• OCCURRENCE Staurolite occurs in Switzerland, Germany, the former USSR, the USA, Brazil, France, and Scotland.

cross shape formed by
• twinned crystals

opaque
• stone

short, black
staurolite
• crystals

CROSS-STONE

CRYSTALS
IN MATRIX

Baguette   Step   Cameo

| SG 3.72 | RI 1.74–1.75 | DR 0.013 | Lustre Vitreous |
|---|---|---|---|

| Crystal structure Orthorhombic | Composition Aluminium iron borosilicate | | Hardness 7 |
|---|---|---|---|

# DUMORTIERITE

Dumortierite is best known in its massive form, which makes an attractive violet and blue decorative stone when polished. Reddish brown and red varieties also occur. Prismatic crystals larger than 1mm (⅛in) are very rare. Dumortierite is also found intergrown with rock crystal (colourless quartz), and is then called dumortierite quartz. This material is usually cut en cabochon or polished to make decorative stones.
• OCCURRENCE Most gem-quality material is found in Nevada (USA). Other localities include France, Madagascar, Norway, Sri Lanka, Canada, Poland, Namibia, and Italy.
• REMARK Dumortierite was named after the French scientist, M.E. Dumortier.

surface may
become pitted
• when polished

distinctive deep
blue colour •

DUMORTIERITE
QUARTZ CABOCHON

CARVED BOTTLE
Hard but attractive, dumortierite is often polished and carved to make decorative objects, like this bottle adorned by the image of a bird.

splintery
surface •

DUMORTIERITE
QUARTZ SLAB

Cabochon   Cameo   Polished

MASSIVE
DUMORTIERITE

| SG 3.28 | RI 1.69–1.72 | DR 0.037 | Lustre Vitreous |
|---|---|---|---|

| Crystal structure Monoclinic | Composition Sodium beryllium phosphate | Hardness 5½ |
|---|---|---|

# BERYLLONITE

Beryllonite crystals are colourless, white, or pale yellow, but its weak fire and low dispersion make it a dull gemstone. In addition, its softness, perfect cleavage, and brittle fracture make it fragile, although with care it may be faceted for collectors.
• OCCURRENCE Beryllonite is a pegmatite mineral, found associated with the minerals phenakite and berylin in Maine in the USA. It is also found in Finland and Zimbabwe, but remains a rare gem.
• REMARK Beryllonite is named after the beryllium content in its chemical composition. It has been confused with other colourless gemstones of low dispersion.

crystals are usually • colourless

weak fire and low dispersion mean gems • appear dull

CUSHION MIXED-CUT

stones are soft and easily • damaged

cleavage planes • visible

Brilliant    Cushion    Pendeloque

CUSHION MIXED-CUT

BERYLLONITE CRYSTAL

| SG 2.83 | RI 1.55–1.56 | DR 0.009 | Lustre Vitreous |
|---|---|---|---|

| Crystal structure Monoclinic | Composition Aluminium sodium hydroxyphosphate | Hardness 5½ |
|---|---|---|

# BRAZILIANITE

Brazilianite is a rare and unusual gemstone. Cut for collectors only, its yellow or yellowish green colour is nonetheless striking. Crystals are fragile and brittle, with conchoidal fracture and perfect cleavage perpendicular to their length.
• OCCURRENCE The main localities are in Brazil, where crystals up to 15cm (6in) have been found. Smaller crystals have been mined in New Hampshire in the USA.
• REMARK Found in Minas Gerais in Brazil in 1944, brazilianite was first thought to be chrysoberyl, but closer examination revealed it to be a completely new mineral. It was named after the country in which it was found, but has since been confused with chrysoberyl, beryl, and topaz.

• distinctive greenish yellow colour

RECTANGULAR STEP-CUT

• stones chip and flaw easily

yellow brazilianite crystals •

apatite crystals •

Cushion    Pendeloque    Baguette

STEP-CUT

GROUP OF CRYSTALS

| SG 2.99 | RI 1.60–1.62 | DR 0.021 | Lustre Vitreous |
|---|---|---|---|

| Crystal structure Monoclinic | Composition Calcium magnesium silicate | Hardness 5½ |
|---|---|---|

# DIOPSIDE

Crystals of diopside may be colourless, but are more usually bottle-green, brownish green, or light green. The more iron-rich and magnesium-poor they are, the darker the colour – almost to black. Very bright green diopside, coloured by chromium, is known as chrome diopside. Violet-blue crystals, coloured by manganese, have been found in Italy and the USA, and may be called violane. It is polished as beads when massive; cut for collectors when transparent; and cut *en cabochon* when fibrous.

• OCCURRENCE Gem-quality chrome diopside is found in Burma, Siberia (Russia), Pakistan, and South Africa. Other diopside localities include Austria, Brazil, Italy, the USA, Madagascar, Canada, and Sri Lanka. Dark green to black diopside, which shows a 4-rayed star when cut *en cabochon*, has been found in southern India since 1964.

*flaws are due to diopside's • fragility*

*chrome diopside variety is bright • emerald-green*

OCTAGONAL STEP-CUT

RECTANGULAR STEP-CUT

*dark green diopside crystals •*

DIOPSIDE IN MATRIX

Brilliant   Baguette   Step   Cabochon

| SG 3.29 | RI 1.66–1.72 | DR 0.029 | Lustre Vitreous |
|---|---|---|---|

| Crystal structure Monoclinic | Composition Hydrated magnesium silicate | Hardness 2½ |
|---|---|---|

# MEERSCHAUM

Meerschaum, also known as sepiolite, is a very fine-grained, soft, light rock. Found as compact, opaque masses with an earthy or chalky appearance, it may be white or grey with a yellowish or reddish tinge. Easily fashioned and often intricately carved, meerschaum is still used in Turkey for bowls for tobacco pipes. With use, the smoke changes the white stone to an attractive yellow colour.

• OCCURRENCE Today the most important source is Eskischehir in Turkey. Other localities include Czechoslovakia, Spain, Greece, and the USA.

• REMARK Light and porous enough to float on water, meerschaum derives its name from the German for sea foam.

BEAD NECKLACE
Soft and light, meerschaum is easy to carve into intricate objects, such as the individually worked beads on this delicate Turkish necklace.

*dull, earthy lustre •*

*light, porous, creamy white meerschaum •*

Bead   Cameo   MASSIVE ROUGH

| SG 1.50 | RI 1.51–1.53 | DR None | Lustre Dull to greasy |
|---|---|---|---|

| Crystal structure Monoclinic | Composition Lithium aluminium silicate | Hardness 7 |
|---|---|---|

# SPODUMENE

Spodumene occurs in a range of colours, although the most common is yellowish grey. Two gem varieties – lilac-pink kunzite (coloured by manganese) and bright emerald-green hiddenite (coloured by chromium) – are very popular with collectors, although perfect cleavage makes them fragile gemstones. Strong pleochroism is easily seen in gem material, showing colourless and two shades of the body colour when viewed from different directions. Stones should always be cut to show the best colour through the table facet. The pink colour may fade with time, but some material is irradiated to intensify it.

• OCCURRENCE Spodumene was discovered in 1877 in Brazil, although it was not until 1879 that kunzite and hiddenite were recognized as different varieties of the same mineral. Spodumene is also found in Madagascar, Burma, the USA, Canada, the former USSR, Mexico, and Sweden.

• REMARK Lilac-pink kunzite is named after the gemmologist G.F. Kunz, who first described it in 1902; hiddenite is named after W.E. Hidden, who discovered it in North Carolina in 1879.

*lilac-pink colour due to • manganese*

*characteristic striations parallel to length •*

CUSHION-CUT KUNZITE

*very pale • green colour*

OCTAGONAL STEP-CUT

KUNZITE CRYSTAL

*emerald-green colour •*

*close-up of hiddenite crystals •*

*• fragments display different colours due to pleochroism*

STEP-CUT HIDDENITE

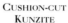

HIDDENITE CRYSTAL FRAGMENTS

*gneiss • matrix*

HIDDENITE CRYSTALS IN MATRIX

| Brilliant | Pendeloque | Step | Step |
|---|---|---|---|

| SG 3.18 | RI 1.66–1.67 | DR 0.015 | Lustre Vitreous |
|---|---|---|---|

| Crystal structure Monoclinic | Composition Calcium aluminium iron hydroxysilicate | Hardness 6½ |
|---|---|---|

# EPIDOTE

This fairly dense, fragile mineral has distinct cleavage and is rarely cut as a gemstone. Crystals are yellow, green, or dark brown columnar prisms, with faces finely striated parallel to the crystal's length. Pleochroism is strong, showing either yellow, green, or brown. Rock made up mainly of epidote may be polished or tumbled and sold as "unakite".
• OCCURRENCE Dark green crystals occur in the Austrian and French Alps. Epidote is also found in the former USSR, Italy, the island of Elba (Italy), Mozambique, and Mexico.

• stones are fragile and easily flawed

*dark brown colour* • **MIXED-CUT**

*columnar epidote* • *crystals*

*parallel* • *striations*

Cushion    Step

**RECTANGULAR TABLE-CUT**

**EPIDOTE CRYSTALS IN MATRIX**

| SG 3.40 | RI 1.74–1.78 | DR 0.035 | Lustre Vitreous |
|---|---|---|---|

| Crystal structure Monoclinic | Composition Calcium titanium silicate | Hardness 5 |
|---|---|---|

# TITANITE

Titanite, also referred to as sphene, is known for its strong fire (its dispersion is higher than that of diamond) and rich colours, but it is seldom used in jewellery as it is too brittle and soft. Nevertheless, transparent yellow, green, or brown gem-quality material is cut for collectors. Titanite is strongly pleochroic (showing three different colours), and has high birefringence (seen as doubling of the back facets) and adamantine lustre.
• OCCURRENCE Gem-quality titanite occurs in cavities in metamorphic rocks such as gneiss and schist, and also in granite. Main localities are Austria, Canada, Switzerland, Madagascar, Mexico, and Brazil.

*doubling of* • *back facets due to high birefringence*

• *high dispersion gives facets of varying colours*

**CUSHION MIXED-CUT**

*characteristic wedge-shaped ends* •

*twinned titanite* • *crystals*

**TITANITE RING**
Faceted stones, like this bright yellow brilliant-cut set in gold, have high fire and rich colours.

Brilliant    Baguette    Mixed

**TITANITE CRYSTALS IN MATRIX**

| SG 3.53 | RI 1.84–2.03 | DR 0.120 | Lustre Adamantine |
|---|---|---|---|

| Crystal structure Monoclinic | Composition Potassium aluminium silicate | Hardness 6 |
|---|---|---|

# COLOURLESS ORTHOCLASE

Orthoclase, an alkali feldspar, occurs in a range of colours, the most common being colourless. Adularia, a colourless, transparent variety from Adular-Bergstock in Switzerland, has a bluish white "schiller" or sheen, called adularescence.
• OCCURRENCE Orthoclase feldspar occurs in intrusive igneous rocks and is one of the main constituents of granitic pegmatites. It is also found in metamorphic rocks such as schist and gneiss. Clear, colourless orthoclase occurs in Madagascar. Yellow and colourless cuttable material, cat's-eyes, and some star stones occur in the gem gravels of Sri Lanka and Burma.
• REMARK Feldspars are the most common rock-forming minerals at the Earth's surface. They are divided into two groups: the alkali feldspars and the plagioclase feldspars (see p.130). Orthoclase derives its name from the Greek for "break straight", a reference to the stone's perfect cleavage at near 90 degrees.

colourless, transparent stone •

ADULARIA CUSHION-CUT

internal cracks • or flaws

ADULARIA CRYSTAL

white orthoclase crystals •

Brilliant

Mixed

ORTHOCLASE WITH QUARTZ

| SG 2.56 | RI 1.51–1.54 | DR 0.005 | Lustre Vitreous |
|---|---|---|---|

| Crystal structure Monoclinic | Composition Potassium aluminium silicate | Hardness 6 |
|---|---|---|

# YELLOW ORTHOCLASE

The yellow variety of orthoclase feld-spar (see colourless orthoclase above) is usually faceted as a step-cut, because the stones are often fragile. The yellow colour is due to the presence of iron. Orthoclase crystals are columnar or tabular prisms, and are often twinned.
• OCCURRENCE The best yellow orthoclase is found in Madagascar in pegmatites, and may be faceted for the collector. Yellow orthoclase from Madagascar and Germany may be cut *en cabochon* to show the cat's-eye effect.
• REMARK Feldspars form in igneous and metamor-phic rocks. Which type is formed depends on the temperature it forms at, and how it cools.

• step-cut is most common, due to fragility of stone

crystals may be translucent to semi-translucent •

Step

RECTANGULAR STEP-CUT

CRYSTAL FRAGMENT

| SG 2.56 | RI 1.51–1.54 | DR 0.005 | Lustre Vitreous |
|---|---|---|---|

| Crystal structure Monoclinic | Composition Potassium aluminium silicate | Hardness 6 |
|---|---|---|

# MOONSTONE (ORTHOCLASE)

milky opalescence
on table facet •

Moonstone is the opalescent variety of orthoclase, with a blue or white sheen (or "schiller"), rather like the shine of the moon after which it is named. This is caused by the reflection of light from the internal structure, made up of alternating layers of albite and ortho-clase feldspar. Thin albite layers give an attractive blue; thicker layers produce a white "schiller". Stones of large size and fine quality are rare.
• OCCURRENCE The best material is from Burma and Sri Lanka. Other localities include India, Madagascar, Brazil, the USA, Mexico, Tanzania, and the European Alps.

**CUSHION BRILLIANT-CUT**

pitted surface
has frosted glass
appearance •

**BLUE MOON**
The moonstone in this finely detailed cameo has a distinct blue "schiller". Moon-worshippers through the ages have used it in their jewellery.

**WATERWORN PEBBLE**

Cushion        Cabochon        Cameo

| SG 2.57 | RI 1.52–1.53 | DR 0.005 | Lustre Vitreous |
|---|---|---|---|

| Crystal structure Triclinic | Composition Potassium aluminium silicate | Hardness 6 |
|---|---|---|

# MICROCLINE

amazonite may be
confused with jade
• or turquoise

characteristic blue-
green colour •

A form of alkali feldspar, microcline may be colourless, white, yellow, pink, red, grey, green, or blue-green. However, the semi-opaque, blue-green variety called amazonite (named after the Amazon River) is most commonly used in jewellery, and may be cut, usually *en cabochon*, up to almost any size. Its striking colour is due to the presence of lead.
• OCCURRENCE The most important source of amazonite is in India. Other localities include the USA, Canada, the former USSR, Madagascar, Tanzania and Namibia.
• REMARK Although microcline has the same composition as ortho-clase, its crystal structure is triclinic.

some surfaces
have silky
• lustre

**AMAZONITE CABOCHON**

polished surface
shows cleavage
• planes

blue, massive
• material

**AMAZONITE SLAB**

**AMAZONITE ROUGH**

Bead        Cabochon        Cameo

| SG 2.56 | RI 1.52–1.53 | DR 0.008 | Lustre Vitreous to silky |
|---|---|---|---|

| Crystal structure Monoclinic | Composition Sodium aluminium silicate | Hardness 7 |
|---|---|---|

# JADEITE (JADE)

For centuries jade was thought to be a single gemstone, but in 1863 two types were recognized: jadeite and nephrite. Nephrite (opposite) is more common, but both are tough, fine-grained rocks, suitable for carving. Jadeite, made up of interlocking, granular pyroxene crystals, occurs in a wide range of colours including green, lilac, white, pink, brown, red, blue, black, orange, and yellow. The most prized variety, imperial jade, is a rich emerald-green, due to chromium. Jadeite commonly has a dimpled surface when polished.

• OCCURRENCE Jadeite is found in metamorphic rocks and as alluvial pebbles and boulders. Some boulders develop a brown skin, due to weathering, and this is often incorporated into carvings and worked pieces. The most important source of jade is Burma, which has supplied China with translucent imperial jade for over 200 years. Historically, Guatemala was an important source of jade, providing the material for the carvings of the Central American Indians. Jadeite also occurs in Japan and California (USA).

• REMARK The Spanish *conquistadores* adopted the use of jadeite when they invaded Central America, and often wore amulets made from it. They called it *piedra de hijada* (loin stone) or *piedra de los rinones* (kidney stone), believing it prevented or cured hip and kidney complaints.

*black inclusions* •    *characteristic emerald-green* • *colour*

POLISHED IMPERIAL JADE

MEXICAN MASK
This opaque, mottled green mask was probably carved in Mexico, prior to 1753. Older jadeite carvings have a characteristic pitted surface; modern abrasives give a smoother finish.

*massive habit* •

*mottled jadeite, fashioned and* • *polished*

*violet colour caused by traces of iron* •

Bead    Cameo    Polished

JADEITE SPHERE

POLISHED SLAB

| SG 3.33 | RI 1.66–1.68 | DR 0.012 | Lustre Greasy to pearly |
|---|---|---|---|

| Crystal structure Monoclinic | Composition Calcium magnesium iron silicate | Hardness 6½ |
| --- | --- | --- |

# NEPHRITE (JADE)

Nephrite, recognized as a separate type of jade since 1863 (see opposite), is found as aggregates of fibrous amphibole crystals. These form an interlocking structure tougher than steel, hence nephrite's popularity as a material for carving – first for weapons and later for ornaments. Colours vary from a dark green, iron-rich nephrite to a cream-coloured, magnesium-rich variety. Nephrite jade may be homogeneous in colour, blotchy, or banded.

• OCCURRENCE Nephrite jade has been carved by the Chinese for over 2,000 years, although the raw material was probably imported first from Turkestan in Central Asia, and later from Burma. Other localities include Siberia (dark green boulders, often with black spots), Russia (spinach-coloured stones), and China itself. Nephrite jade is also found in various rocks in the North and South Islands of New Zealand (pieces carved in the 17th century include Maori clubs called *meres*). Other localities include Australia (black nephrite), the USA, Canada, Mexico, Brazil, Taiwan, Zimbabwe (dark green), Italy, Poland, Germany, and Switzerland.

• REMARK Nephrite may be confused with bowenite serpentine, may be imitated by composite stones, or dyed to improve colour.

CHINESE CARVING
Nephrite jade has been carved in China for centuries, and is tough enough to be worked into intricate designs. China is still one of the world's main cutting centres.

DAGGER HANDLE
Because of its great strength, nephrite has been used since prehistoric times to make weapons. In fact at one time it was known as "axe stone".

*colour may be blotchy* •

FABERGÉ SNAIL
The greasy lustre of nephrite jade enhances this witty carving by the famous Russian jeweller, Fabergé.

*tough, interlocking structure* •

CHINESE CAMEL
The shape of the original boulder has been integrated into the design of this carving. Only one side of the boulder has been fashioned.

Bead

Cameo

Polished

NEPHRITE BOULDER

| SG 2.96 | RI 1.61–1.63 | DR 0.027 | Lustre Greasy to pearly |
| --- | --- | --- | --- |

| Crystal structure Monoclinic | Composition Copper hydroxycarbonate | Hardness 4 |
|---|---|---|

# MALACHITE

Malachite is usually found in opaque green masses; the colour is due to the copper content. Crystals are too small for faceting, but the massive material is carved or polished in many ways to reveal the alternating bands of light and dark green. In the past, malachite was worn to ward off danger and illness.
• OCCURRENCE Malachite occurs in small quantities worldwide, but in larger quantities in copper-mining areas. Zaire is the most important producer.

• *concentric green to near-black banding*

*common botryoidal habit*

Cabochon

**POLISHED MALACHITE**

**MALACHITE ROUGH**

| SG 3.80 | RI 1.85 (mean) | DR 0.025 | Lustre Vitreous to silky |
|---|---|---|---|

| Crystal structure Monoclinic | Composition Hydrated copper silicate | Hardness 2 |
|---|---|---|

# CHRYSOCOLLA

Chrysocolla usually occurs as a bright green or bluish crust, or as compact, grape-like groups. Crystals intergrown with quartz or with opal are more commonly used in jewellery.
• OCCURRENCE Copper-mining areas, particularly Chile, the former USSR, and Zaire. "Eilat Stone" (intergrown with malachite and turquoise) reputedly came from King Solomon's mines.

• *brown patches of copper ore*

*crystals are very small (micro-crystalline)*

Bead

**POLISHED CHRYSOCOLLA**

**CHRYSOCOLLA ROUGH**

| SG 2.20 | RI 1.57–1.63 | DR 0.030 | Lustre Greasy to vitreous |
|---|---|---|---|

| Crystal structure Monoclinic | Composition Copper hydroxycarbonate | Hardness 3½ |
|---|---|---|

# AZURITE

Azurite is an azure-blue copper mineral, occasionally found as prismatic crystals (rarely faceted), but more usually in massive form intergrown with malachite.
• OCCURRENCE Found particularly in copper-mining areas such as Australia, Chile, the former USSR, Africa, and China. Stones from Chessy, near Lyons in France, are called chessylite.

• *bands of green malachite*

• *polished stone*

*dark blue azurite crystals*

Cameo

**BANDED CHESSYLITE**

**AZURITE CRYSTALS ON MATRIX**

• *green malachite*

| SG 3.77 | RI 1.73–1.84 | DR 0.110 | Lustre Vitreous |
|---|---|---|---|

| Crystal structure Monoclinic | Composition Magnesium hydroxysilicate | Hardness 5 |
|---|---|---|

# SERPENTINE

The name serpentine refers to a group of predominantly green minerals that occur in masses of tiny intergrown crystals. The two main types used in jewellery are bowenite (translucent green or blue-green) and the rarer williamsite (translucent, oily green, veined or spotted with inclusions). They may be carved, engraved, or polished. Various marbles also contain serpentine veins.

• OCCURRENCE Bowenite is found in New Zealand, China, Afghanistan, South Africa, and the USA; Williamsite occurs in Italy, England, and China.

*characteristic patches formed by inclusions*

*partly translucent*

*rock composed of various serpentine minerals*

WILLIAMSITE
CABOCHON

*lack of colour due to thinness of slice*

Cameo

Polished

BOWENITE PENDANT

SERPENTINITE
ROCK

| SG 2.60 | RI 1.55–1.56 | DR 0.001 | Lustre Vitreous to greasy |
|---|---|---|---|

| Crystal structure Monoclinic | Composition Hydrated zinc phosphate | Hardness 3½ |
|---|---|---|

# PHOSPHOPHYLLITE

This is one of the rarest of gem-stones, and is highly prized by collectors. The crystals, which are prismatic or with a thick, tabular habit, range from colourless to deep bluish green, but the best specimens are a very delicate bluish green. Nevertheless, phosphophyllite is rarely cut, as the material is brittle and fragile, and large crystals are too valuable to be broken up.

• OCCURRENCE The finest crystals, and the only ones to be faceted, are from Bolivia. Other localities include Germany and New Hampshire (USA).

*pale blue-green colour is most sought-after*

*cuttable material mainly from Bolivia*

RECTANGULAR STEP-CUT

*small fragments can be faceted*

*crystals crack easily*

STEP-CUT

*phosphophyllite crystals*

PHOSPHOPHYLLITE CRYSTALS

PHOSPHOPHYLLITE
CRYSTALS ON PYRITE

Brilliant

Step

| SG 3.10 | RI 1.59–1.62 | DR 0.021 | Lustre Vitreous |
|---|---|---|---|

| Crystal structure Monoclinic | Composition Magnesium aluminium hydroxyphosphate | Hardness 5½ |
|---|---|---|

# LAZULITE

Crystals of lazulite are rare. Colours vary from a mottled pale blue to dark blue. Transparent stones are pleochroic, showing blue and colourless, but often lazulite is not transparent. Semi-translucent or opaque stones, found as small crystal fragments, may be polished, carved, or tumbled to make beads or decorative stones.
• OCCURRENCE Localities include the USA, Brazil, India, Sweden, Austria, Switzerland, Madagascar, and Angola.

blue and white
• mottling

bipyramidal
lazulite
crystal •

POLISHED CABOCHON

Cabochon

LAZULITE
IN MATRIX

| SG 3.10 | RI 1.61–1.64 | DR 0.031 | Lustre Vitreous |
|---|---|---|---|

| Crystal structure Monoclinic | Composition Hydrated calcium borosilicate | Hardness 3½ |
|---|---|---|

# HOWLITE

Howlite is a soft, light mineral with a chalky white colour, commonly with black or brown veins. Crystals are occasionally found in groups. It is very porous and may be dyed to imitate other minerals, especially turquoise.
• OCCURRENCE Howlite has been found in large quantities in California (USA).
• REMARK Even though it is soft, howlite will withstand a polish, and is occasionally used as a decorative stone.

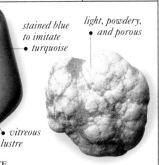
stained blue
to imitate
• turquoise

light, powdery,
• and porous

• vitreous
lustre

STAINED HOWLITE

Bead

MASSIVE ROUGH

| SG 2.58 | RI 1.58–1.59 | DR 0.022 | Lustre Vitreous |
|---|---|---|---|

| Crystal structure Monoclinic | Composition Hydrated calcium sulphate | Hardness 2 |
|---|---|---|

# GYPSUM

Several varieties of gypsum are used as decorative stones. The most important, alabaster, is found as fine-grained masses in pastel shades, but is commonly stained in stronger colours. Selenite is colourless, occasionally cut for collectors, but very soft. Satin spar is a fibrous variety, polished or cut *en cabochon*. Rose shapes (called "desert rose") also occur.
• OCCURRENCE Localities include Italy and England (alabaster); Italy, Mexico, the USA, and Chile (selenite).

cat's-eye
• effect

parallel
fibrous
structure •

• satin
lustre

POLISHED
SATIN SPAR

Cabochon

SATIN SPAR ROUGH

| SG 2.32 | RI 1.52–1.53 | DR 0.010 | Lustre Silky to vitreous |
|---|---|---|---|

| Crystal structure Monoclinic | Composition Calcium hydroxyborosilicate | Hardness 5 |
|---|---|---|

# DATOLITE

Transparent, colourless crystals of datolite are cut for the collector only. A tinge of yellow, green, or white may also be present. More often, however, datolite occurs as a massive material, which may contain copper inclusions.
• **OCCURRENCE** Localites include Austria, Italy, Norway, the USA, Germany, and England. The main source of massive datolite with inclusions is the Lake Superior area of North America.

crystals are cut for collectors only •

colourless, with tinge of yellow •

OCTAGONAL STEP-CUT

Step

CRYSTAL

| SG 2.95 | RI 1.62–1.65 | DR 0.044 | Lustre Vitreous |
|---|---|---|---|

| Crystal structure Monoclinic | Composition Lithium aluminium silicate | Hardness 6 |
|---|---|---|

# PETALITE

Fine petalite is rare and fragile. For this reason it is only occasionally cut for the collector. Crystals are transparent, colourless or white, occurring as tabular or columnar prisms with a glassy appearance. Massive petalite is more common, cut *en cabochon*.
• **OCCURRENCE** Elba (Italy), Brazil, Australia, Sweden, Finland, USA, Zimbabwe, and Namibia.

*fine stones are* • *rare and fragile*

*fibrous, massive material* •

CUSHION MIXED-CUT

Cushion

PETALITE ROUGH

| SG 2.42 | RI 1.50–1.51 | DR 0.014 | Lustre Vitreous to pearly |
|---|---|---|---|

| Crystal structure Monoclinic | Composition Beryllium aluminium hydroxysilicate | Hardness 7½ |
|---|---|---|

# EUCLASE

Euclase is a rare gem. The most attractive colour is a pale aquamarine blue, but it also occurs in white, green, and colourless forms. Crystals are prismatic with a perfect cleavage, which means they are fragile and must be cut and handled with care.
• **OCCURRENCE** Euclase occurs mainly in pegmatites. Localities include Brazil, Tanzania, Zaire, Kenya, the former USSR, India, Zimbabwe, and the USA.

black mineral • inclusions

striated • prism

SQUARE STEP-CUT

Step

*conchoidal fracture* •

PRISMATIC CRYSTAL

| SG 3.10 | RI 1.65–1.67 | DR 0.019 | Lustre Vitreous |
|---|---|---|---|

| Crystal structure Triclinic | Composition Sodium calcium aluminosilicate | Hardness 6 |
|---|---|---|

# ALBITE

Albite is one of six species in the plagioclase feldspar series. Each species is
defined by its albite and anorthite
content: albite itself has the highest albite
content. It is usually white, though gems
are often colourless. Peristerite, an
albite-oligoclase mix, has a
blue sheen, like moon-
stone (see p.123).
• OCCURRENCE
The best peristerite
is from Canada.

*albite is
usually
• colourless*

*cream-coloured,
• opaque crystals*

Brilliant    Brilliant

**MIXED-CUT**

**ALBITE CRYSTALS**

| SG 2.64 | RI 1.54–1.55 | DR 0.009 | Lustre Vitreous to pearly |
|---|---|---|---|

| Crystal structure Triclinic | Composition Sodium calcium aluminosilicate | Hardness 6 |
|---|---|---|

# OLIGOCLASE

Oligoclase is a species of plagioclase
feldspar (see above). The variety used
in jewellery is called sunstone or, less
commonly, aventurine feldspar. It has
reflective inclusions of red, orange, or
green platy crystals, which give it a
metallic glitter. Sunstone may be faceted or carved – often as cabochons.
• OCCURRENCE Sunstone
occurs in metamorphic and
igneous rocks in Norway, the
USA, India, the former
USSR, and Canada.

**SUNSTONE PIN**
The bright
spangles in this
cabochon, set
as a tie-pin,
are caused by
tiny inclusions
of hematite.

*hematite flakes
produce sparkling
parallel bands •*

Cabochon

**SUNSTONE ROUGH**

| SG 2.64 | RI 1.54–1.55 | DR 0.007 | Lustre Vitreous |
|---|---|---|---|

| Crystal structure Triclinic | Composition Sodium calcium aluminosilicate | Hardness 6 |
|---|---|---|

# LABRADORITE

Labradorite is the plagioclase
feldspar (see albite, above) most
commonly faceted as a gem. It
occurs in orange, yellow, colourless, and red, but the material that
shows a play of colour, or "schiller", is
the most popular for use in jewellery.
• OCCURRENCE Occurs in
metamorphic and igneous
rocks in Labrador
(Canada), Finland,
Norway, and the
former USSR.

*play of colour
(schiller) seen
on polished
• surface*

*interference
of light at
junctions of
internal
• structures*

**CABOCHON**

Cabochon    Polished

**LABRADORITE
ROUGH**

| SG 2.70 | RI 1.56–1.57 | DR 0.010 | Lustre Vitreous |
|---|---|---|---|

| Crystal structure Triclinic | Composition Hydrated copper aluminium phosphate | Hardness 6 |
|---|---|---|

# TURQUOISE

One of the first gemstones to be mined, turquoise has long been prized for its intense colour, which varies from sky-blue to green, depending on the quantities of iron and copper within it. Turquoise is commonly found in microcrystalline, massive form, usually as encrustations, in veins, or as nodules. It is opaque to semi-translucent, light and very fragile, with conchoidal fracture. Some material is very porous, leading to fading and cracking, so it may be impregnated with wax or resin to maintain its appearance.
• OCCURRENCE Sky-blue turquoise from Iran is generally regarded as the most desirable, but in Tibet a greener variety is preferred. Localities in Mexico and the USA produce a greener, more porous material that tends to fade more quickly. Other localities include the former USSR, Chile, Australia, Turkestan, and Cornwall (England).
• REMARK Turquoise has been thought to warn the wearer of danger or illness by changing colour. It has been imitated by stained howlite, fossil bone or tooth, limestone, chalcedony, glass, and enamel. In 1972, an imitation turquoise was produced in France by Gilson.

**GREEN FACE**
This greenish blue turquoise stone has been carved in the image of a child's face, set in relief in a swivel ring.

**PERSIAN BLUE**
These two ornaments, engraved and inlaid with gold, are made from the finest sky-blue turquoise, mined in Persia (now Iran) for over 3,000 years. The distinctive colour is due to the presence of copper and traces of iron. Persian turquoise was introduced to Europe via Turkey – hence its name, derived from the word "turkish".

*pattern engraved and inlaid with gold*

*cut and polished as cabochon*

*laboratory-made stone has uniform colour*

*"spiderweb" turquoise has black veins*

*intense blue-green colour*

**GILSON "SPIDERWEB" IMITATION**

**GILSON IMITATION**

| Bead | Cabochon | Cameo |
|---|---|---|

*thin crust of turquoise on matrix*

**TURQUOISE IN MATRIX**

| SG 2.80 | RI 1.61–1.65 | DR 0.040 | Lustre Waxy to dull |
|---|---|---|---|

| Crystal structure Triclinic | Composition Manganese silicate | Hardness 6 |
|---|---|---|

# RHODONITE

Rhodonite has a distinct pink or rose-red colour, although material containing black veins is more popular than a uniform pink. Massive rhodonite is usually opaque to translucent, and is carved, or cut as cabochons or beads. Transparent crystals are rare and fragile, but some have been cut for collectors.
• OCCURRENCE Both crystals and massive material have been found in the Urals (Russia), Sweden, and Australia. Other localities for fine-grained rhodonite include Brazil, Mexico, the USA, Canada, Italy, India, Madagascar, South Africa, Japan, New Zealand, and England.
• REMARK The name comes from *rhodos*, the Greek for "rose", referring to the distinct colour.

black-veined stones are the most • popular

• characteristic pink-red colour

OVAL CABOCHON

massive habit •

Bead  Cabochon  Cameo

black areas rich • in manganese

RHODONITE ROUGH

| SG 3.60 | RI 1.71–1.73 | DR 0.014 | Lustre Vitreous |
|---|---|---|---|

| Crystal structure Triclinic | Composition Lithium aluminium hydroxyphosphate | Hardness 6 |
|---|---|---|

# AMBLYGONITE

Amblygonite is found in a wide range of colours from white, pink, green, and blue to golden yellow and, more rarely, colourless. Large, transparent to translucent crystals may occur, but, as amblygonite is relatively soft, they are cut solely for collectors. Amblygonite is also found as cleavable or compact masses.
• OCCURRENCE Amblygonite is found in pegmatites. Brazil is the source of most gem-quality material, but it is also found in the USA. A pale mauve variety occurs in Namibia.
• REMARK Amblygonite has been confused with brazilianite and scapolite.

dark yellow • colour

• stones are too soft to be popular for jewellery

OVAL BRILLIANT-CUT

straw-yellow colour is most common •

pale yellow • colour

OVAL BRILLIANT-CUT

perfect cleavage •

INCOMPLETE CRYSTAL

Brilliant  Brilliant  Mixed

| SG 3.02 | RI 1.57–1.60 | DR 0.026 | Lustre Vitreous |
|---|---|---|---|

| Crystal structure Triclinic | Composition Complex borosilicate | Hardness 7 |
|---|---|---|

# AXINITE

Axinite gets its name from its sharp-edged, axehead-shaped crystals. Although attractive and hard, they are brittle and rarely flawless, and faceted for collectors only. Brown is the most usual colour, although it also occurs in honey-yellow and plum-purple varieties. A rare Tanzanian axinite is blue. Axinite is strongly pleochroic.
• **OCCURRENCE** Axinite is found in cavities in granite and in metamorphic rocks. Localities include New Jersey (USA), where the attractive honey-yellow crystals are found, Mexico, Cornwall (England), France, and in the gem gravels of Sri Lanka.
• **REMARK** Darker axinite has been confused with smoky quartz.

iron gives stone its rich brown colour

OVAL STEP-CUT

fragile, sharp-edged crystals

pale blue colour due to low iron content

Brilliant    Brilliant    Mixed

BRILLIANT-CUT

AXINITE CRYSTALS

| SG 3.28 | RI 1.67–1.70 | DR 0.011 | Lustre Vitreous |
|---|---|---|---|

| Crystal structure Triclinic | Composition Aluminium silicate | Hardness 5 or 7 |
|---|---|---|

# KYANITE

Gem-quality kyanite crystals are pale to deep blue, or white, grey, or green. Colour distribution in crystals may be uneven, with darker blue patches towards the interior.
• **OCCURRENCE** Kyanite is found in metamorphic gneiss and schist, and in pegmatite veins through metamorphic rocks. It may be weathered out into alluvial deposits. Gem-quality crystals are found in Burma, Brazil, Kenya, and the European Alps. Alluvial deposits are found in India, Australia, and Kenya, and in several localities in the USA.
• **REMARK** Kyanite crystals have two hardness values: they are softer parallel to the direction of cleavage, and harder perpendicular to it.

cracks due to formation at high pressure

rich blue colour

uneven colour distribution

RECTANGULAR STEP-CUT

staurolite crystals commonly occur with kyanite

kyanite crystals

CRYSTAL

CRYSTALS IN MATRIX

Baguette    Step    Cabochon

| SG 3.68 | RI 1.71–1.73 | DR 0.017 | Lustre Vitreous to pearly |
|---|---|---|---|

| Crystal structure Amorphous | Composition Hydrated silica gel | Hardness 6 |
|---|---|---|

# OPAL

Opal is a hardened silica gel, usually containing 5–10 per cent water. It is therefore non-crystalline, unlike most other gemstones, and may eventually dry out and crack. There are two varieties: precious opal, which shows flashes of colour (iridescence), depending on the angle of viewing; and common or "potch" opal, which is often opaque and displays no iridescence. The iridescence of precious opal is caused by the way the structure, a regular arrangement of tiny silica spheres, diffracts light – the larger the spheres, the greater the range of colours. Precious opal occurs in a number of colour varieties, some of which are shown here.

• OCCURRENCE Opal fills cavities in sedimentary rocks, or veins in igneous rocks. It forms stalagmites or stalactites, and replaces organic material in fossil wood, shell, and bone. Australia has been the main producer of opals since the 19th century. Other localities include Czechoslovakia, the USA, Brazil, Mexico, and southern Africa.

• REMARK Opals have been imitated by Slocum stone, a tough, man-made glass, and in 1973 Gilson made an imitation opal in the laboratory (see p.36).

precious opal with dark background is called black opal

cracks due to loss of original water content

**BLACK PRECIOUS OPAL**

high-quality black opal from Australia

matrix

**BLACK PRECIOUS OPAL IN MATRIX**

good-quality stones are transparent, not milky

beautiful, rich orange body colour gives fire opal its name

**FIRE OPAL BRILLIANT**

**FIRE OPAL RING**
Although many opals are cut *en cabochon*, this transparent fire opal has been faceted as an octagonal step-cut, and set in a gold ring.

volcanic rhyolite matrix

transparent fire opal

opaque white opal

**OPAL IN MATRIX**

| SG 2.10 | RI 1.37–1.47 | DR None | Lustre Vitreous |
|---|---|---|---|

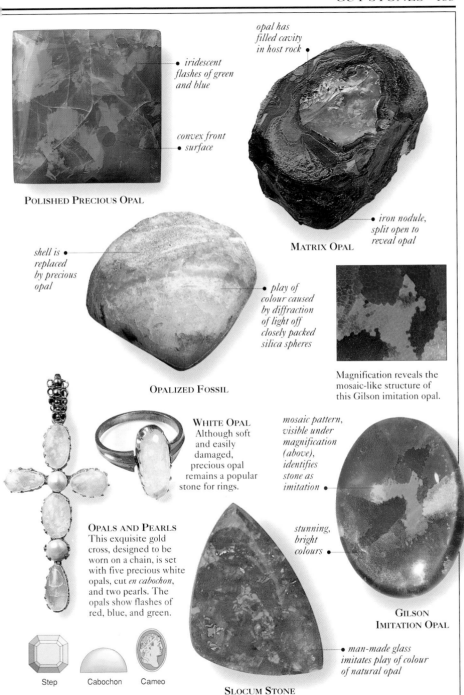

iridescent
flashes of green
and blue

opal has
filled cavity
in host rock

convex front
surface

**POLISHED PRECIOUS OPAL**

iron nodule,
split open to
reveal opal

**MATRIX OPAL**

shell is
replaced
by precious
opal

play of
colour caused
by diffraction
of light off
closely packed
silica spheres

Magnification reveals the
mosaic-like structure of
this Gilson imitation opal.

**OPALIZED FOSSIL**

**WHITE OPAL**
Although soft
and easily
damaged,
precious opal
remains a popular
stone for rings.

mosaic pattern,
visible under
magnification
(above),
identifies
stone as
imitation

**OPALS AND PEARLS**
This exquisite gold
cross, designed to be
worn on a chain, is set
with five precious white
opals, cut *en cabochon*,
and two pearls. The
opals show flashes of
red, blue, and green.

stunning,
bright
colours

Step     Cabochon     Cameo

**GILSON
IMITATION OPAL**

man-made glass
imitates play of colour
of natural opal

**SLOCUM STONE**

| Crystal structure Amorphous | Composition Mainly silicon dioxide | Hardness 5 |
|---|---|---|

# OBSIDIAN

Obsidian is a natural glass. It is formed from volcanic lava that cooled too quickly for significant crystallization to occur. Hence it is amorphous, with no cleavage; fracture is conchoidal. Obsidian is usually black, but brown, grey, and, more rarely, red, blue, and green material is found. The colour may be uniform, striped, or spotted. Some inclusions give obsidian a metallic sheen, while internal bubbles or crystals (called crystallites) produce a "snowflake" effect (hence snowflake obsidian) or an iridescence seen as flashes of colour.

• OCCURRENCE Obsidian is found in areas where there is, or has been, volcanic activity: for example, Hawaii (USA), Japan, and Java. Other localities include Iceland, Hungary, the Lipari Islands off Italy, the former USSR, Mexico, Ecuador, and Guatemala. Dark nodules found in Arizona and New Mexico (USA) are called "Apache tears".

• REMARK Obsidian has been used since prehistoric times for making tools, weapons, masks, mirrors, and jewellery. The very sharp shards of the natural glass have been fashioned as blades, arrowheads, and daggers. Today most obsidian jewellery comes from North and Central America.

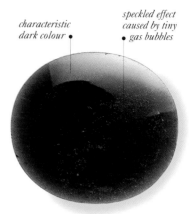

*characteristic dark colour* • 
*speckled effect caused by tiny* • *gas bubbles*

**OBSIDIAN CABOCHON**

*rare red* • *obsidian*

*banding caused by solidification of flowing* • *lava*

**POLISHED OBSIDIAN SLICE**

*polished specimen has smooth, glassy* • *surface*

*rough specimen has uneven surface* •

**APACHE TEARS**

*mineral-lined cavities, called spherules* •

*amorphous black obsidian* •

Cabochon

Polished

**OBSIDIAN ROUGH**

| SG 2.35 | RI 1.48–1.51 | DR None | Lustre Vitreous |
|---|---|---|---|

| Crystal structure Amorphous | Composition Mainly silicon dioxide | Hardness 5 |
| --- | --- | --- |

# TEKTITES

The first tektites were found in 1787 in the Moldau River in Czechoslovakia, hence their original name of "moldavites". Other colour varieties of this natural glass have since been found in many different localities. Tektites are usually translucent, and occur in a range of colours from green to brown. Their surfaces are usually uneven or rough, with a distinctive lumpy, jagged, or scarred texture. Tektites do not contain the crystallites found in obsidian (opposite). They may, however, have characteristic inclusions of round or torpedo-shaped bubbles or treacle-like swirls.

• OCCURRENCE The Moldau River in Czechoslovakia is now the only known locality for green, transparent tektite. Tektites from Thailand have been carved as small, decorative objects, worn in the belief that they give protection from evil.

• REMARK Several ideas have been put forward to explain the mysterious origin of tektites. One theory is that they came to Earth from outer space, melting as they passed through the atmosphere and thus forming their characteristic shape and surface texture. A second theory is that the impact of a large meteorite caused the surrounding rocks to melt and scatter, with cracks and scars then appearing as they cooled.

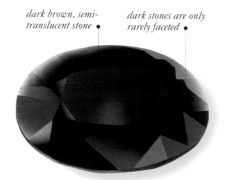

*dark brown, semi-translucent stone*

*dark stones are only rarely faceted*

**OVAL BRILLIANT-CUT**

*button shape caused by way molten glass has cooled*

*surface shows cooling cracks*

**TEKTITE ROUGH**

*tektite varieties are named after their place of origin*

**AUSTRALITE ROUGH**

*stone may be confused with diopside due to green colour*

*green, transparent material is most suitable for faceting*

*distinctive craggy, uneven surface*

**MOLDAVITE BRILLIANT-CUT**

*translucent and transparent in parts*

Brilliant

Cushion

Bead

**MOLDAVITE ROUGH**

| SG 2.40 | RI 1.48–1.51 | DR None | Lustre Vitreous |
| --- | --- | --- | --- |

| Crystal structure Orthorhombic | Composition Calcium carbonate, conchiolin, and water | Hardness 3 |
|---|---|---|

# PEARL

Pearls are formed in shellfish – especially oysters and mussels – as a natural defence against an irritant, such as a piece of grit. Layers of aragonite, known as nacre, are secreted around the irritant, and gradually build up to form the solid pearl. Light reflecting from these overlapping layers produces a characteristic iridescent lustre, also known as the "orient of pearl". In cultured pearls an irritant is introduced to initiate the formation of a pearl. In a "nucleated" cultured pearl a small bead is used as the nucleus, upon which the layers of nacre are secreted. Pearls vary in colour from white, white with a hint of colour (often pink), to brown or black, depending on the type of mollusc and the water. They are sensitive to acids, dryness, and humidity, and so are less durable than many other gems.
• OCCURRENCE Natural pearls have been harvested from the Persian Gulf, the Gulf of Manaar (Indian Ocean), and the Red Sea for thousands of years. The coasts of Polynesia and Australia produce mainly cultured pearls. Both freshwater and saltwater pearls are cultivated in Japan and China. Freshwater pearls occur in the rivers of Scotland, Ireland, France, Austria, Germany, and Mississippi (USA).
• REMARK Pearls were once thought to be the tears of the gods.

pearl colour is a mixture of body colour and lustre

pearl of Strombus gigas

NATURAL PINK PEARL

pearl of Tridacna gigas

NATURAL WHITE PEARL

brick-coloured where attached to shell

pearls form as spheres when irritant is not attached to shell

pinkish tinge

NATURAL FRESHWATER PEARLS

shell of the pearl oyster (Pinctada maxima)

irregular shapes may develop if irritant is attached to shell

natural white pearl

mother-of-pearl lining

iridescent, "pearly" lustre

NATURAL FRESHWATER PEARLS

NATURAL PEARL IN OYSTER SHELL

| SG 2.71 | RI 1.53–1.68 | DR Not applicable | Lustre Pearly |
|---|---|---|---|

**A "BOMBAY BUNCH"**
For hundreds of years Bombay (in India) has been an important centre for the buying and selling of pearls. To present them for selling, pearls are sorted by size, then strung into bunches on silk thread.

*different sizes are included so that a complete necklace can be made from a "bunch"* •

*pearl buddhas formed on casts placed* • *inside shell*

**BUDDHA PEARLS**
To produce miniature images of the Buddha, tiny casts were placed into the shell of this pearl mussel (*Cristaria plicata*). The mussel laid down nacreous layers over the casts, forming "blister" pearls. The pearls are later removed and the backs hidden in the mount or covered with mother-of-pearl.

**JAPANESE CULTURE**
This necklace, made by the Mikimoto company of Japan, uses saltwater cultured pearls. Japan leads the world in the production of cultured pearls, although they have been used by the Chinese for hundreds of years.

• *cultured pearls have the same pearly lustre as natural specimens*

*silver-wire* • *tassels*

Bead

| Crystal structure Amorphous | Composition Variety of lignite | Hardness 2½ |
|---|---|---|

# JET

Jet is organic in origin. Like coal, it was formed from the remains of wood immersed in stagnant water millions of years ago, then compacted and fossilized by the pressures of burial. Jet is black or dark brown, but may contain pyrite inclusions which have a brassy colour and metallic lustre. Jet takes a good polish, and is often faceted. When burned or touched with a hot needle, it exudes the characteristic smell of coal.

Because jet is organic, it may dry out, causing the surface to crack.

• OCCURRENCE Evidence suggests that jet has been mined since about 1400BC, and worked pieces of jet have been found in prehistoric burial mounds. During the Roman occupation of the British Isles, worked pieces of jet were shipped to Rome. Perhaps the most famous historical source is Whitby in Yorkshire, England, where much of the jet that was so popular for the mourning jewellery of the 19th century originated. During this time the mining and fashioning of jet provided the town with much of its income. Other localities include Spain, France, Germany, Poland, India, Turkey, the former USSR, China, and the USA.

*gems made from jet take a good polish •*

*opaque, with velvety • lustre*

**OVAL CABOCHON**

• REMARK Jet was popular for mourning jewellery in the 19th century due to its sombre colour and modest appearance, and traditionally it has been fashioned into rosaries for monks. Jet has also been known as black amber, as it may induce an electric charge, like that of amber, when rubbed. Powdered jet added to water or wine was believed to have medicinal powers.

*uppermost surface is convex; back is flat •*

*faceting can add life to an otherwise dull gem •*

**ROSE-CUT**

*triangular facets •*

*surface cracks resulting from • dehydration*

*fine-grained, fragile specimen with rough, cracked surfaces •*

*dull, earthy lustre before polishing •*

**DRILLED AND FACETED BEAD**

| SG 1.33 | RI 1.64–1.68 | DR Not applicable | Lustre Velvety to waxy |
|---|---|---|---|

**VICTORIAN EARRINGS**
Jet is light to wear, and so particularly suitable for earrings. During the Victorian era in Britain it was very popular for mourning jewellery.

**BLACK ROSE**
This piece of carved Whitby jet, with a finely wrought rose at the centre, dates from the latter part of the 19th century.

**FOSSIL-BEARING JET**
The ammonite and bivalve fossils trapped in this jet specimen are evidence of its organic origin.

**JET PENDANT**
This exquisite pendant of a dove with a heart in its beak shows how well jet can be carved and polished.

ammonite fossil •

• bivalve fossil

highly polished beads •

**TURKISH BEADS**
This necklace from eastern Turkey is made from beads of polished and drilled jet. The high polish has given the beads an attractive lustre.

Bead          Cameo          Polished

| Crystal structure Trigonal | Composition Calcium carbonate or conchiolin | Hardness 3 |
|---|---|---|

# CORAL

Coral is made up of the skeletal remains of marine animals called coral polyps. These tiny creatures live in colonies which form branching structures as they grow, eventually forming coral reefs and atolls. The surface of these coral "branches" has a distinctive patterning made by the original skeleton – either striped or like wood grain. Most corals – red, pink, white, and blue varieties – are made of calcium carbonate; black and golden corals are made of a horn-like substance called conchiolin. Red coral is the most valuable, and has been used in jewellery for thousands of years. Dull at first, all coral has a vitreous lustre when polished, but is sensitive to heat and acids and may fade with wear. Coral may be imitated by porcelain, stained bone, glass, plastic, or rubber and gypsum mixtures.

- **OCCURRENCE** Most precious coral is found in warm waters. Japanese coral is red, pink, or white. Red and pink coral is also found on the Mediterranean and African coasts, the Red Sea, and the waters off Malaysia and Japan. Black and golden coral is found off the coasts of the West Indies, Australia, and the Pacific islands.
- **REMARK** Coral has been associated with the protection of children, and parents may still give a gift of coral to their young children.

*vivid red colour*

*high polish shows vitreous lustre*

RED CORAL CABOCHON

*polished surface*

*cross-section reveals intricate banded structure*

RED CORAL SLICE

*branches form from coral polyp skeletons*

*red coral from the Mediterranean*

*distinctive "wood grain" pattern on surface of branches*

RED CORAL

RED CORAL CARVING
This piece of red coral (*Corallium rubrum*) from the Mediterranean has been carved to show a monkey climbing a blossoming tree.

| SG 2.68 | RI 1.49–1.66 | DR Not applicable | Lustre Dull to vitreous |
|---|---|---|---|

distinctive
pitted surface •

Heliopora caerules
coral found in seas
• around Philippines

coral colonies
naturally form
branched, tree-
• like structures

black coral is
made from
horn-like
conchiolin •

highly
polished
surface •

• blue coral is
often used to
make beads

oval
cabochon •

BLACK CORAL

BLACK CORAL CABOCHON

BLUE CORAL

imitation slabs may be
carved, polished, or
fashioned as beads •

polished bead
manufactured by
Gilson of France
to imitate dark
pink coral •

IMITATION
CORAL
These beads are
made of vegetable
ivory, stained to
imitate natural pink
coral. Imitations are
generally even in colour
and fail to show the
distinctive "wood grain"
structure of natural coral.

IMITATION
CORAL BEAD

IMITATION CORAL

Bead          Cabochon          Cameo

| Crystal structure Various | Composition Calcium carbonate | Hardness 2½ |
|---|---|---|

# SHELL

Shells come in a wide variety of sizes, shapes, and colours, and may be fashioned into beads, buttons, jewellery, inlay, knife handles, snuff boxes, and other decorative items. Conch shells with pink and white layers may be carved into intricate and attractive cameos, as may helmet shells, which have white outer layers and golden brown or orange inner layers. The large pearl oysters (*Pinctada maxima* and *P. margaritifera*), abalones (paua), and topshells (Trochidae) are all prized for their iridescent (mother-of-pearl) shell linings. Tortoiseshell comes, not from the tortoise, but from the hard shell (carapace) of the Hawksbill Turtle. It has rich brown mottling or flame-like patterns on a warm, translucent, golden yellow background, and is fashioned by warming the shell to flatten it and to scrape off the ridges, followed by polishing and cutting to shape.
• **OCCURRENCE** *Pinctada* oysters are found off northern Australia. Abalones are found off the coasts of the USA and paua shells off New Zealand. The Hawksbill Turtle is found in the warm waters of Indonesia and the West Indies.
• **REMARK** Tortoiseshell has now been largely replaced by plastic imitations.

**TIGER COWRIE CAMEO**
This oriental lady has been carved in a Tiger Cowrie shell (*Cypraea tigris*). The different coloured layers have been cut away to create the effect of foreground and background.

*bright pink interior may be used for inlay work •*

*shell found on inshore sands of Indo-Pacific •*

*• surface layers cut away to leave image in high relief*

**ROMAN CAMEO**
This cameo has been carved into the shell of *Cassidae madagascarensii*. The detail is picked out in the upper layers of the shell.

**SPIDER CONCH**
(*LAMBIS LAMBIS*)

| SG 1.30 | RI 1.53–1.69 | DR Not applicable | Lustre Dull to vitreous |
|---|---|---|---|

**HINGED BOX**
The lid and base of
this box show the
distinctive colouring
and patterning of
tortoiseshell. Some
light areas are
transparent to semi-
translucent; darker
areas are opaque.

When magnified, spots can
be seen in natural, but not
in imitation, tortoiseshell.

*distinctive rich
brown mottling* •

**HAIR COMB**
This tortoise-
shell comb shows
attractive, almost
fiery, patterns of
yellow and
brown, with
darker patches.

*ridges are
scraped away
during
fashioning* •

*iridescent colours
are prized in many
forms of jewellery
and decorative
items* •

*nacreous
lining is used
for jewellery
• and inlays*

**TORTOISESHELL (CARAPACE
OF HAWKSBILL TURTLE)**

**SHELL PILL-BOX**
The inlay in the lid
of this pill-box has
been fashioned
from the layered,
iridescent lining of
a shell from the
Haliotis family of
shellfish.

Cabochon          Cameo          Polished

**MOTHER-OF-PEARL
SHELL**

| Crystal structure Amorphous | Composition Calcium hydroxyphosphate and organic | Hardness 2½ |
|---|---|---|

# IVORY

Ivory has been prized for thousands of years for its rich, creamy colour, its fine texture, and its ease of carving. Until quite recently it was a popular material for both jewellery and ornaments, but international restrictions on trading now help to protect the animals from which ivory can be taken. The teeth or tusks of mammals all have ivory as a constituent. Although usually associated with elephants, ivory from the Hippopotamus, Wild Boar, and Warthog is also used. Marine mammals such as the Sperm Whale, Walrus, Sea Lion, and Narwhal provide ivory as well. Fossil ivory – from prehistoric animals such as mammoths, mastodons, or dinosaurs – can also be carved.

• OCCURRENCE The best ivory is from the African Elephant. It has a warm tint and little grain or mottling. Ivory from the Indian Elephant is a denser white, softer, and easier to work, but yellows more easily. Other sources of ivory include Europe, Burma, and Indonesia.

• REMARK The use of ivory simulants – bone, horn, jasper, vegetable ivory, plastic, and resin – has been strongly encouraged in order to protect ivory-bearing animals. Ivory carving has a long history: one piece of carved mammoth ivory found in France is estimated to be over 30,000 years old. In China and Japan it remains highly valued, even today.

**INDIAN ELEPHANT IVORY**
This intricately fashioned scene was probably carved from the tusk of an Indian Elephant, whose ivory is softer and whiter than the African Elephant's.

*distinctive curved growth • lines*

*thin canals containing nerve fibres •*

**AFRICAN ELEPHANT IVORY**
Made from warm, mellow African Elephant ivory, this Roman head is worked in the style popular in the 4th to 5th century BC.

*cut and polished molar tooth •*

**ELEPHANT IVORY CUP**
Looking down into this cup, the criss-crossing, curving pattern unique to elephant ivory is visible.

**POLISHED SECTION OF ELEPHANT TOOTH**

| SG 1.90 | RI 1.53–1.54 | DR Not applicable | Lustre Dull to greasy |
|---|---|---|---|

**DRILLED BONE**
Bone may be used as an ivory simulant. These two pieces have been worked as buttons or beads, with a plain back and carved front.

outer surface has yellowed with time •

radial lines •

**SECTION OF HIPPOPOTAMUS TUSK**

• surface of Sperm Whale ivory yellows with age

**WALRUS IVORY**
This necklace is made from stained walrus ivory. Ivory is porous, and readily takes a dye.

green-stained beads are intended to • imitate jade

tough outer rim surrounds concentric inner • structure

**PART OF WHALE TOOTH**

fruit of the • doom palm

**VEGETABLE IVORY**
This necklace is made of polished and drilled vegetable ivory beads, given a pale, artificial stain to imitate coral. Imitation ivory is now encouraged, as more and more ivory-bearing animals face premature extinction.

beads stained pink to imitate coral •

Bead

Cameo

Polished

hard, creamy white nut • used to imitate elephant and other ivories

**VEGETABLE IVORY IN SHELL**

| Crystal structure Amorphous | Composition Mixture of organic plant resins | Hardness 2½ |
|---|---|---|

# AMBER

Amber is the fossilized resin of trees. Most amber is golden yellow to golden orange, but green, red, violet, and black amber has been found. Transparent to translucent, it usually occurs as nodules or small, irregularly shaped masses, often with a cracked and weathered surface. Amber may contain insects (and more rarely frogs, toads, and lizards), moss, lichen, or pine needles that were trapped millions of years ago while the resin was still sticky. Air bubbles may give amber a cloudy appearance, but heating in oil will clear this. When rubbed, amber produces a negative electrical charge that attracts dust. "Ambroid" is formed by heating and pressing together scraps of amber.

• OCCURRENCE The most famous deposits are in the Baltic region, particularly along the coasts of Poland and the former USSR. Baltic amber (known as succinite) washed from the seabed may reach as far as the coasts of England, Norway, and Denmark. Amber from Burma is called burmite; Sicilian amber is known as simetite. Other localities include the Dominican Republic, Mexico, France, Spain, Italy, Germany, Romania, Canada, Czechoslovakia, and the USA.

• REMARK Amber has had a number of medicinal uses attributed to it, but today is used almost exclusively for jewellery. It has been imitated by plastic, glass, synthetic resin, and other natural resins, like copal.

characteristic golden orange colour •

resinous lustre •

transparent • bead

POLISHED BEADS

cracks produce spangling effect •

cracks may be caused by heat • treatment

• cloudy, opaque area

POLISHED SUN-SPANGLED BEAD

weathered surface •

• transparent area

PARTLY POLISHED AMBER

pebble found washed up on beach •

BALTIC AMBER ROUGH

| SG 1.08 | RI 1.54–1.55 | DR Not applicable | Lustre Resinous |
|---|---|---|---|

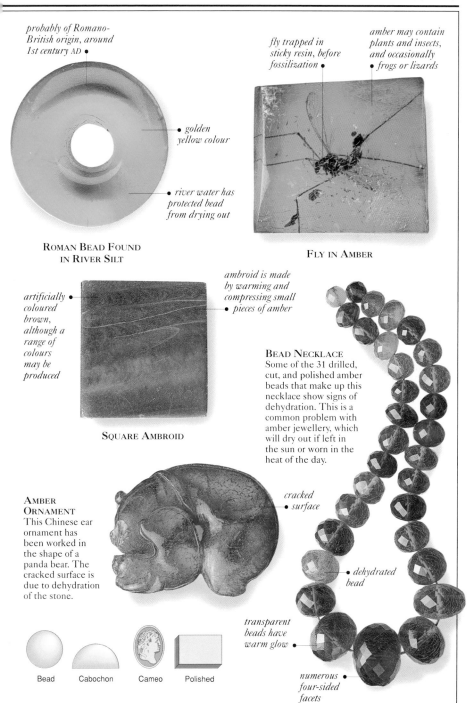

*probably of Romano-British origin, around 1st century AD*

*golden yellow colour*

*river water has protected bead from drying out*

**ROMAN BEAD FOUND IN RIVER SILT**

*fly trapped in sticky resin, before fossilization*

*amber may contain plants and insects, and occasionally frogs or lizards*

**FLY IN AMBER**

*artificially coloured brown, although a range of colours may be produced*

*ambroid is made by warming and compressing small pieces of amber*

**SQUARE AMBROID**

**BEAD NECKLACE**
Some of the 31 drilled, cut, and polished amber beads that make up this necklace show signs of dehydration. This is a common problem with amber jewellery, which will dry out if left in the sun or worn in the heat of the day.

**AMBER ORNAMENT**
This Chinese ear ornament has been worked in the shape of a panda bear. The cracked surface is due to dehydration of the stone.

*cracked surface*

*dehydrated bead*

*transparent beads have warm glow*

*numerous four-sided facets*

Bead  Cabochon  Cameo  Polished

# TABLE OF PROPERTIES

THIS TABLE BRINGS TOGETHER all the technical information for each gem species, arranged alphabetically by gem name. By so doing, it is intended to give the reader an at-a-glance reference to the more important physical and optical properties of each gem species.

The chemical composition of each gem is shown here by a formula, which includes all essential elements of that gem. Composition may vary slightly, depending on locality and conditions of formation. The physical properties of the gems – their hardness and specific gravity – are given as mean (average) values. Hardness is denoted by a figure from Mohs' scale of hardness, a scale used to classify the hardness of minerals relative to one another. The intervals between successive values are unequal, and an intermediate value such as 3½ denotes that the hardness is between 3 and 4, but it is not necessarily exactly halfway between. Hardness may vary slightly depending upon exact chemical content, so a mean figure is given here. The values for specific gravity (SG) give an indication of the density of a gem, and are also given as mean figures.

The optical properties of the gems are represented here by the refractive indices (RI) and the birefringence (DR).

They are related to crystal structure: a gem with cubic structure has a single value as its refractive index (RI); doubly refracting gems have two refractive indices (see p.21). Doubly refracting gems also have a value of birefringence (DR), found by using a refractometer. This figure is the difference between the highest and the lowest refractive indices. Physical and optical properties are continually reviewed, as new minerals are discovered and new deposits exploited, so all figures given here are mean values, to be used as a guide only.

## KEY TO CHEMICAL ELEMENTS IN THIS BOOK

| | | | |
|---|---|---|---|
| Al | ALUMINIUM | Mg | MAGNESIUM |
| Ag | SILVER | Mn | MANGANESE |
| Au | GOLD | Na | SODIUM |
| B | BORON | O | OXYGEN |
| Ba | BARIUM | P | PHOSPHORUS |
| Be | BERYLLIUM | Pb | LEAD |
| C | CARBON | Pt | PLATINUM |
| Ca | CALCIUM | S | SULPHUR |
| Cl | CHLORINE | Si | SILICON |
| Cr | CHROMIUM | Sn | TIN |
| Cu | COPPER | Sr | STRONTIUM |
| F | FLUORINE | Ti | TITANIUM |
| Fe | IRON | W | TUNGSTEN |
| H | HYDROGEN | Zn | ZINC |
| K | POTASSIUM | Zr | ZIRCONIUM |
| Li | LITHIUM | | |

| NAME & CHEMICAL COMPOSITION | STRUCTURE | HARDNESS | SG | RI | DR |
|---|---|---|---|---|---|
| ACHROITE (TOURMALINE) $Na(Li,Al)_3Al_6(BO_3)_3Si_6O_{18}(OH)_4$ | Trigonal | 7½ | 3.06 | 1.62–1.64 | 0.018 |
| AGATE (CHALCEDONY) $SiO_2$ | Trigonal | 7 | 2.61 | 1.53–1.54 | 0.004 |
| ALBITE $(Na,Ca)AlSi_3O_8$ | Triclinic | 6 | 2.64 | 1.54–1.55 | 0.009 |
| ALMANDINE (GARNET) $Fe_3Al_2(SiO_4)_3$ | Cubic | 7½ | 4.00 | 1.76–1.83 | None |
| AMBER mainly $C_{10}H_{16}O$ | Amorphous | 2½ | 1.08 | 1.54–1.55 | N/A |

| NAME & CHEMICAL COMPOSITION | STRUCTURE | HARDNESS | SG | RI | DR |
|---|---|---|---|---|---|
| AMBLYGONITE $LiAl(F,OH)PO_4$ | Triclinic | 6 | 3.02 | 1.57–1.60 | 0.026 |
| AMETHYST (QUARTZ) $SiO_2$ | Trigonal | 7 | 2.65 | 1.54–1.55 | 0.009 |
| ANDALUSITE $Al_2SiO_5$ | Orthorhombic | 7½ | 3.16 | 1.63–1.64 | 0.010 |
| ANDRADITE GARNET $Ca_3Fe_2(SiO_4)_3$ | Cubic | 6½ | 3.85 | 1.85–1.89 | None |
| ANGLESITE $PbSO_4$ | Orthorhombic | 3 | 6.35 | 1.87–1.89 | 0.017 |
| APATITE $Ca(F,Cl)Ca_4(PO_4)_3$ | Hexagonal | 5 | 3.20 | 1.63–1.64 | 0.003 |
| AQUAMARINE (BERYL) $Be_3Al_2(SiO_3)_6$ | Hexagonal | 7½ | 2.69 | 1.57–1.58 | 0.006 |
| ARAGONITE $CaCO_3$ | Orthorhombic | 3½ | 2.94 | 1.53–1.68 | 0.155 |
| AVENTURINE QUARTZ $SiO_2$ | Trigonal | 7 | 2.65 | 1.54–1.55 | 0.009 |
| AXINITE $CaFeMgBAl_2Si_4O_{15}(OH)$ | Triclinic | 7 | 3.28 | 1.67–1.70 | 0.011 |
| AZURITE $Cu_3(OH)_2(CO_3)_2$ | Monoclinic | 3½ | 3.77 | 1.73–1.84 | 0.110 |
| BARYTE $BaSO_4$ | Orthorhombic | 3 | 4.45 | 1.63–1.65 | 0.012 |
| BENITOITE $BaTiSi_3O_9$ | Hexagonal | 6½ | 3.67 | 1.76–1.80 | 0.047 |
| BERYLLONITE $NaBePO_4$ | Monoclinic | 5½ | 2.83 | 1.55–1.56 | 0.009 |
| BLOODSTONE (CHALCEDONY) $SiO_2$ | Trigonal | 7 | 2.61 | 1.53–1.54 | 0.004 |
| BRAZILIANITE $Al_3Na(PO_4)_2(OH)_4$ | Monoclinic | 5½ | 2.99 | 1.60–1.62 | 0.021 |
| BROWN QUARTZ (SMOKY QUARTZ) $SiO_2$ | Trigonal | 7 | 2.65 | 1.54–1.55 | 0.009 |
| CALCITE $CaCO_3$ | Trigonal | 3 | 2.71 | 1.48–1.66 | 0.172 |
| CARNELIAN (CHALCEDONY) $SiO_2$ | Trigonal | 7 | 2.61 | 1.53–1.54 | 0.004 |
| CASSITERITE $SnO_2$ | Tetragonal | 6½ | 6.95 | 2.00–2.10 | 0.100 |
| CELESTINE $SrSO_4$ | Orthorhombic | 3½ | 3.98 | 1.62–1.63 | 0.010 |
| CERUSSITE $PbCO_3$ | Orthorhombic | 3½ | 6.51 | 1.80–2.08 | 0.274 |
| CHALCEDONY $SiO_2$ | Trigonal | 7 | 2.61 | 1.53–1.54 | 0.004 |
| CHATOYANT QUARTZ $SiO_2$ | Trigonal | 7 | 2.65 | 1.54–1.55 | 0.009 |
| CHRYSOBERYL $BeAl_2O_4$ | Orthorhombic | 8½ | 3.71 | 1.74–1.75 | 0.009 |

| Name & Chemical Composition | Structure | Hardness | SG | RI | DR |
|---|---|---|---|---|---|
| CHRYSOCOLLA<br>$(Cu,Al)_2H_2Si_2O_5(OH)_4.nH_2O$ | Monoclinic | 2 | 2.20 | 1.57–1.63 | 0.030 |
| CHRYSOPRASE (CHALCEDONY)<br>$SiO_2$ | Trigonal | 7 | 2.61 | 1.53–1.54 | 0.004 |
| CITRINE (QUARTZ)<br>$SiO_2$ | Trigonal | 7 | 2.65 | 1.54–1.55 | 0.009 |
| CORAL<br>$CaCO_3$ (or $C_3H_{48}N_9O_{11}$) | Trigonal | 3 | 2.68 | 1.49–1.66 | N/A |
| DANBURITE<br>$CaB_2(SiO_4)_2$ | Orthorhombic | 7 | 3.00 | 1.63–1.64 | 0.006 |
| DATOLITE<br>$Ca(B,OH)SiO_4$ | Monoclinic | 5 | 2.95 | 1.62–1.65 | 0.044 |
| DIAMOND<br>C | Cubic | 10 | 3.52 | 2.42 | None |
| DIOPSIDE<br>$CaMg(SiO_3)_2$ | Monoclinic | 5½ | 3.29 | 1.66–1.72 | 0.029 |
| DIOPTASE<br>$CuOSiO_2H_2O$ | Trigonal | 5 | 3.31 | 1.67–1.72 | 0.053 |
| DOLOMITE<br>$CaMg(CO_3)_2$ | Trigonal | 3½ | 2.85 | 1.50–1.68 | 0.179 |
| DRAVITE (TOURMALINE)<br>$NaMg_3Al_6(BO_3)_3Si_6O_{18}(OH)_4$ | Trigonal | 7½ | 3.06 | 1.61–1.63 | 0.018 |
| DUMORTIERITE<br>$Al_7(BO_3)(SiO_4)_3O_3$ | Orthorhombic | 7 | 3.28 | 1.69–1.72 | 0.037 |
| EMERALD (BERYL)<br>$Be_3Al_2(SiO_3)_6$ | Hexagonal | 7½ | 2.71 | 1.57–1.58 | 0.006 |
| ENSTATITE<br>$Mg_2Si_2O_6$ | Orthorhombic | 5½ | 3.27 | 1.66–1.67 | 0.010 |
| EPIDOTE<br>$Ca_2(Al,Fe)_3(OH)(SiO_4)_3$ | Monoclinic | 6½ | 3.40 | 1.74–1.78 | 0.035 |
| EUCLASE<br>$Be(Al,OH)SiO_4$ | Monoclinic | 7½ | 3.10 | 1.65–1.67 | 0.019 |
| FIRE AGATE (CHALCEDONY)<br>$SiO_2$ | Trigonal | 7 | 2.61 | 1.53–1.54 | 0.004 |
| FLUORITE<br>$CaF_2$ | Cubic | 4 | 3.18 | 1.43 | None |
| GOLD<br>Au | Cubic | 2½ | 19.30 | None | None |
| GOSHENITE (BERYL)<br>$Be_3Al_2(SiO_3)_6$ | Hexagonal | 7½ | 2.80 | 1.58–1.59 | 0.008 |
| GROSSULAR (GARNET)<br>$Ca_3Al_2(SiO_4)_3$ | Cubic | 7 | 3.49 | 1.69–1.73 | None |
| GYPSUM<br>$CaSO_4.2H_2O$ | Monoclinic | 2 | 2.32 | 1.52–1.53 | 0.010 |
| HAMBERGITE<br>$Be_2(OH)BO_3$ | Orthorhombic | 7½ | 2.35 | 1.55–1.63 | 0.072 |
| HAUYNE<br>$(Na,Ca)_{4-8}Al_6Si_6(O,S)_{24}(SO_4Cl)_{1-2}$ | Cubic | 6 | 2.40 | 1.50 (mean) | None |
| HELIODOR (BERYL)<br>$Be_3Al_2(SiO_3)_6$ | Hexagonal | 7½ | 2.80 | 1.57–1.58 | 0.005 |

| NAME & CHEMICAL COMPOSITION | STRUCTURE | HARDNESS | SG | RI | DR |
|---|---|---|---|---|---|
| HEMATITE $Fe_2O_3$ | Trigonal | 6½ | 5.20 | 2.94–3.22 | 0.280 |
| HESSONITE (GROSSULAR GARNET) $Ca_3Al_2(SiO_4)_3$ | Cubic | 7¼ | 3.65 | 1.73–1.75 | None |
| HOWLITE $C_2B_5SiO_9(OH)_5$ | Monoclinic | 3½ | 2.58 | 1.58–1.59 | 0.022 |
| HYPERSTHENE $(Fe,Mg)SiO_3$ | Orthorhombic | 5½ | 3.35 | 1.65–1.67 | 0.010 |
| INDICOLITE (TOURMALINE) $Na(Li,Al)_3Al_6(BO_3)_3Si_6O_{18}(OH)_4$ | Trigonal | 7½ | 3.06 | 1.62–1.64 | 0.018 |
| IOLITE $Mg_2Al_4Si_5O_{18}$ | Orthorhombic | 7 | 2.63 | 1.53–1.55 | 0.010 |
| IVORY $Ca_5(PO_4)_3(OH)$ and organic material | Amorphous | 2½ | 1.90 | 1.53–1.54 | N/A |
| JADEITE (JADE) $Na(Al,Fe)Si_2O_6$ | Monoclinic | 7 | 3.33 | 1.66–1.68 | 0.012 |
| JASPER (CHALCEDONY) $SiO_2$ | Trigonal | 7 | 2.61 | 1.53–1.54 | 0.004 |
| JET Lignite | Amorphous | 2½ | 1.33 | 1.64–1.68 | N/A |
| KORNERUPINE $Mg_4(Al,Fe)_6(Si,B)_4O_{21}(OH)$ | Orthorhombic | 6½ | 3.32 | 1.66–1.68 | 0.013 |
| KYANITE $Al_2SiO_5$ | Triclinic | 5 or 7 | 3.68 | 1.71–1.73 | 0.017 |
| LABRADORITE $(Na,Ca)(Al,Si)_4O_8$ | Triclinic | 6 | 2.70 | 1.56–1.57 | 0.010 |
| LAPIS LAZULI (LAZURITE) $(Na,Ca)_8(Al,Si)_{12}O_{24}(SO_4)Cl_2(OH)_2$ | Various | 5½ | 2.80 | 1.50 (mean) | None |
| LAZULITE $MgAl_2(PO_4)_2(OH)_2$ | Monoclinic | 5½ | 3.10 | 1.61–1.64 | 0.031 |
| MALACHITE $Cu_2(OH)_2CO_3$ | Monoclinic | 4 | 3.80 | 1.85 (mean) | 0.025 |
| MEERSCHAUM $Mg_4Si_6O_{15}(OH)_2.6H_2O$ | Monoclinic | 2½ | 1.50 | 1.51–1.53 | None |
| MICROCLINE $KAlSi_3O_8$ | Triclinic | 6 | 2.56 | 1.52–1.53 | 0.008 |
| MILKY QUARTZ $SiO_2$ | Trigonal | 7 | 2.65 | 1.54–1.55 | 0.009 |
| MOONSTONE (ORTHOCLASE) $KAlSi_3O_8$ | Monoclinic | 6 | 2.57 | 1.52–1.53 | 0.005 |
| MORGANITE (BERYL) $Be_3Al_2(SiO_3)_6$ | Hexagonal | 7½ | 2.80 | 1.58–1.59 | 0.008 |
| NEPHRITE (JADE) $Ca_2(Mg,Fe)_5Si_8O_{22}(OH)_2$ | Monoclinic | 6½ | 2.96 | 1.61–1.63 | 0.027 |
| OBSIDIAN Mainly $SiO_2$ | Amorphous | 5 | 2.35 | 1.48–1.51 | None |
| OLIGOCLASE $(Na,Ca)(Al,Si)_4O_8$ | Triclinic | 6 | 2.64 | 1.54–1.55 | 0.007 |
| ONYX $SiO_2$ | Trigonal | 7 | 2.61 | 1.53–1.54 | 0.004 |

| Name & Chemical Composition | Structure | Hardness | SG | RI | DR |
|---|---|---|---|---|---|
| OPAL<br>$SiO_2.nH_2O$ | Amorphous | 6 | 2.10 | 1.37–1.47 | None |
| ORTHOCLASE<br>$KAlSi_3O_8$ | Monoclinic | 6 | 2.56 | 1.51–1.54 | 0.005 |
| PADPARADSCHA (CORUNDUM)<br>$Al_2O_3$ | Trigonal | 9 | 4.00 | 1.76–1.77 | 0.008 |
| PEARL<br>$CaCO_3,C_3H_{18}N_9O_{11}.nH_2O$ | Orthorhombic | 3 | 2.71 | 1.53–1.68 | N/A |
| PERIDOT<br>$(Mg,Fe)_2SiO_4$ | Orthorhombic | 6½ | 3.34 | 1.64–1.69 | 0.036 |
| PETALITE<br>$Li_2OAl_2O_38SiO_2$ | Monoclinic | 6 | 2.42 | 1.50–1.51 | 0.014 |
| PHENAKITE<br>$Be_2SiO_4$ | Trigonal | 7½ | 2.96 | 1.65–1.67 | 0.015 |
| PHOSPHOPHYLLITE<br>$Zn_2(Fe,Mn)(PO_4)_2.4H_2O$ | Monoclinic | 3½ | 3.10 | 1.59–1.62 | 0.021 |
| PLASMA (CHALCEDONY)<br>$SiO_2$ | Trigonal | 7 | 2.61 | 1.53–1.54 | 0.004 |
| PLATINUM<br>$Pt$ | Cubic | 4 | 21.40 | None | None |
| PRASE (CHALCEDONY)<br>$SiO_2$ | Trigonal | 7 | 2.61 | 1.53–1.54 | 0.004 |
| PREHNITE<br>$Ca_2Al_2Si_3O_{10}(OH)_2$ | Orthorhombic | 6 | 2.87 | 1.61–1.64 | 0.016 |
| PYRITE<br>$FeS_2$ | Cubic | 6 | 4.90 | None | None |
| PYROPE (GARNET)<br>$Mg_3Al_2(SiO_4)_3$ | Cubic | 7¼ | 3.80 | 1.72–1.76 | None |
| RHODOCHROSITE<br>$MnCO_3$ | Trigonal | 4 | 3.60 | 1.60–1.80 | 0.220 |
| RHODONITE<br>$(Mn,Fe,Mg,Ca)SiO_3$ | Triclinic | 6 | 3.60 | 1.71–1.73 | 0.014 |
| ROCK CRYSTAL (QUARTZ)<br>$SiO_2$ | Trigonal | 7 | 2.65 | 1.54–1.55 | 0.009 |
| ROSE QUARTZ<br>$SiO_2$ | Trigonal | 7 | 2.65 | 1.54–1.55 | 0.009 |
| RUBELLITE (TOURMALINE)<br>$Na(Li,Al)_3Al_6(BO_3)_3Si_6O_{18}(OH)_4$ | Trigonal | 7½ | 3.06 | 1.62–1.64 | 0.018 |
| RUBY (CORUNDUM)<br>$Al_2O_3$ | Trigonal | 9 | 4.00 | 1.76–1.77 | 0.008 |
| RUTILE<br>$TiO_2$ | Tetragonal | 6 | 4.25 | 2.62–2.90 | 0.287 |
| SAPPHIRE (CORUNDUM)<br>$Al_2O_3$ | Trigonal | 9 | 4.00 | 1.76–1.77 | 0.008 |
| SARD<br>$SiO_2$ | Trigonal | 7 | 2.61 | 1.53–1.54 | 0.004 |
| SARDONYX (CHALCEDONY)<br>$SiO_2$ | Trigonal | 7 | 2.61 | 1.53–1.54 | 0.004 |
| SCAPOLITE<br>$Na_4Al_3Si_9O_{24}Cl–Ca_4Al_6Si_6O_{24}(CO_3,SO_4)$ | Tetragonal | 6 | 2.70 | 1.54–1.58 | 0.020 |

| Name & Chemical Composition | Structure | Hardness | SG | RI | DR |
|---|---|---|---|---|---|
| SCHEELITE $CaWO_4$ | Tetragonal | 5 | 6.10 | 1.92–1.93 | 0.017 |
| SCHORL (TOURMALINE) $NaFe_3Al_6(BO_3)_3Si_6O_{18}(OH)_4$ | Trigonal | 7½ | 3.06 | 1.62–1.67 | 0.018 |
| SERPENTINE $Mg_6(OH)_8Si_4O_{10}$ | Monoclinic | 5 | 2.60 | 1.55–1.56 | 0.001 |
| SHELL $CaCO_3$ and $C_{32}H_{48}N_2O_{11}$ | Various | 2½ | 1.30 | 1.53–1.69 | N/A |
| SILLIMANITE $Al_2SiO_5$ | Orthorhombic | 7½ | 3.25 | 1.66–1.68 | 0.019 |
| SILVER $Ag$ | Cubic | 2½ | 10.50 | None | None |
| SINHALITE $Mg(Al,Fe)BO_4$ | Orthorhombic | 6½ | 3.48 | 1.67–1.71 | 0.038 |
| SMITHSONITE $ZnCO_3$ | Trigonal | 5 | 4.35 | 1.62–1.85 | 0.230 |
| SODALITE $3NaAlSiO_4NaCl$ | Cubic | 5½ | 2.27 | 1.48 (mean) | None |
| SPESSARTINE (GARNET) $Mn_3Al_2(SiO_4)_3$ | Cubic | 7 | 4.16 | 1.79–1.81 | None |
| SPHALERITE $(Zn,Fe)S$ | Cubic | 3½ | 4.09 | 2.36–2.37 | None |
| SPINEL $MgAl_2O_4$ | Cubic | 8 | 3.60 | 1.71–1.73 | None |
| SPODUMENE $LiAl(SiO_3)_2$ | Monoclinic | 7 | 3.18 | 1.66–1.67 | 0.015 |
| STAUROLITE $(Fe,Mg,Zn)_2Al_9(Si,Al)_4O_{22}(OH)_2$ | Orthorhombic | 7 | 3.72 | 1.74–1.75 | 0.013 |
| TAAFFEITE $BeMg_3Al_8O_{16}$ | Hexagonal | 8 | 3.61 | 1.72–1.77 | 0.004 |
| TEKTITES Mainly $SiO_2$ | Amorphous | 5 | 2.40 | 1.48–1.51 | None |
| TITANITE (SPHENE) $CaTiSiO_5$ | Monoclinic | 5 | 3.53 | 1.84–2.03 | 0.120 |
| TOPAZ $Al_2(F,OH)_2SiO_4$ | Orthorhombic | 8 | 3.54 | 1.62–1.63 | 0.010 |
| TUGTUPITE $Na_4AlBeSi_4O_{12}Cl$ | Tetragonal | 6 | 2.40 | 1.49–1.50 | 0.006 |
| TURQUOISE $CuAl_6(PO_4)_4(OH)_8.5H_2O$ | Triclinic | 6 | 2.80 | 1.61–1.65 | 0.040 |
| UVAROVITE (GARNET) $Ca_3Cr_2(SiO_4)_3$ | Cubic | 7½ | 3.77 | 1.86–1.87 | None |
| VESUVIANITE (IDOCRASE) $Ca_6Al(Al,OH)(SiO_4)_5$ | Tetragonal | 6½ | 3.40 | 1.70–1.75 | 0.005 |
| WATERMELON TOURMALINE $Na(Li,Al)_3Al_6(BO_3)_3Si_6O_{18}(OH)_4$ | Trigonal | 7½ | 3.06 | 1.62–1.64 | 0.018 |
| ZIRCON $ZrSiO_4$ | Tetragonal | 7½ | 4.69 | 1.93–1.98 | 0.059 |
| ZOISITE $Ca_2(Al,OH)Al_2(SiO_4)_3$ | Orthorhombic | 6½ | 3.35 | 1.69–1.70 | 0.010 |

# GLOSSARY

WORDS PRINTED in bold type have their own definition elsewhere in the glossary.

• **ABSORPTION SPECTRUM**
Pattern of dark lines or bands seen when a gem is viewed through a **spectroscope**.

• **ALLOCHROMATIC**
Refers to gems coloured by impurities, without which the gem would be colourless.

• **ALLUVIAL DEPOSITS**
Concentrations of material that have been separated by weathering from the host **rock**, then deposited by rivers or streams.

• **AMORPHOUS**
Without a regular internal atomic structure or external shape.

• **ASSOCIATED MINERALS**
Minerals found growing together, though not necessarily **intergrown**.

• **ASTERISM**
Star effect seen on some stones when cut *en cabochon*.

• **BASAL PINACOID**
Feature relating to **crystal** symmetry. A **columnar** or **prismatic** crystal with flat ends may be referred to as having a basal pinacoid.

• **BIREFRINGENCE (DR)**
The difference between the highest and the lowest **refractive indices** in **doubly refractive** gems.

• **BOTRYOIDAL**
Shape similar to a bunch of grapes.

• **CABOCHON**
Gem cut and polished to have a domed upper surface. Such stones are said to be cut *en cabochon*.

• **CAMEO**
Design in low relief, around which the background has been cut away.

• **CARAT (CT)**
Unit of weight used for gems – a carat is one-fifth of a gram. It is also used to describe the purity of gold – pure gold is 24 carat.

• **CHATOYANCY**
The cat's-eye effect shown by some stones when cut *en cabochon*.

• **CLEAVAGE**
Breaking of a stone along lines of weakness related to the internal atomic structure. *See also* **Fracture**.

• **COLUMNAR**
Type of **habit** in which **crystals** form in the shape of columns (elongated prisms).

• **COMPOSITE STONE**
Stone assembled from several pieces, often to imitate a gem.

• **CONCHOIDAL FRACTURE**
Shell-like fracture. *See* **Fracture**.

• **CROWN**
Top part of a cut stone, above the **girdle**.

• **CRYPTOCRYSTALLINE**
**Mineral** structure in which **crystals** are so small they are not distinguishable with a microscope.

• **CRYSTAL**
Solid that has a definite internal atomic structure, producing a characteristic external shape and physical and optical properties.

• **CRYSTAL STRUCTURE**
Internal atomic structure of a **crystal**. All crystalline gems may be classified in one of seven groups, according to the symmetry of their structure: cubic, tetragonal, hexagonal, trigonal, orthorhombic, monoclinic, and triclinic.

• **CUT**
Term used to describe the way in which a **stone** is faceted. *See also* **Faceting**.

• **DICHROIC**
Refers to a gem that appears two different colours or shades when viewed from different directions.

• **DIFFRACTION**
The splitting of white light into its constituent spectral colours – the colours of the rainbow – when it passes through a hole or grating.

• **DISPERSION**
The splitting of white light into its constituent spectral colours – the rainbow colours – when it passes through inclined surfaces, such as those on a **prism** or **faceted** gem. Dispersion in gems is called fire.

• **DOUBLE REFRACTION (DR)**
Phenomenon in which each ray of light is split in two as it enters a non-cubic **mineral**. Each ray travels at a different speed and has its own **refractive index**. *See also* **Birefringence**.

• **DOUBLET**
**Composite stone** made of two pieces cemented or glued together.

• **EVAPORITE DEPOSIT**
**Sedimentary rock** or **mineral** resulting from the evaporation of water from mineral-bearing fluids, usually sea water.

• **FACES**
Flat surfaces that make up the external shape of a **crystal**.

• **FACET**
Surface of a cut and polished gem.

• **FACETING**
Cutting and polishing of the surfaces of a **gemstone** into **facets**. The number and shape of the facets give the stone its style of **cut**.

• **FANCY-CUT**
Name applied to a stone given an unconventional shape when cut.

• **FIRE**
*See* **Dispersion**.

• **FRACTURE**
Chipping or breaking of a stone in a way unconnected to the internal atomic structure. Because of this, fracture surfaces are usually uneven. *See also* **Cleavage**.

• **GEMSTONE**
Decorative material, usually a **mineral**, prized for some or all of the qualities of beauty, durability, and rarity. It is used synonymously with "gem" and "stone" throughout this book.

• **GEODE**
Cavity within a **rock**, in which **crystals** line the inner surface and grow towards the centre.

• **GIRDLE**
Band around the widest part of a cut stone, where the **crown** meets the **pavilion**.

• **GRANITE**
Coarse-grained **igneous rock** comprising mainly quartz, feldspar, and mica.

• **HABIT**
Shape in which a **crystal** naturally occurs.

• **HARDNESS**
*See* **Mohs' Scale of Hardness**.

• **HEAT TREATMENT**
Application of heat to a gem with the purpose of enhancing the colour or clarity.

• **HYDROTHERMAL**
Refers to processes that involve the alteration or deposition of minerals by water heated by igneous activity.

• **IDIOCHROMATIC**
Describes gems whose colour is due to elements that are an essential part of their chemical composition.

• **IGNEOUS ROCKS**
**Rocks** formed from erupted volcanic **lava** or solidified **magma**.

- **IMITATION GEMSTONE**
Material that has the outward appearance of the gem it is intended to imitate, but which has different physical properties. *See also* **Synthetic gemstone**.
- **INCLUSIONS**
Markings or foreign bodies found within a stone. Some can be used to identify a particular **species**.
- **INTAGLIO**
Design in which the subject is cut lower than the background.
- **INTERGROWN**
When two or more **minerals** grow together and become interlocked.
- **INTRUSIVE**
**Igneous rock** that has solidified within other rocks, below the Earth's surface.
- **IRIDESCENCE**
Reflection of light off internal features in a gem, giving rise to rainbow-like play of colours.
- **LAPIDARY**
Craftsman who cuts and polishes gemstones.
- **LAVA**
Molten **rock** erupted from volcanoes. *See also* **Magma**.
- **LUSTRE**
Shine or "look" of a gemstone due to reflection of light off the surface.
- **MAGMA**
**Rock** in a molten state below the Earth's surface. *See also* **Lava**.
- **MAMMILLATED**
Smooth, rounded shape.
- **MASSIVE**
Used to describe **minerals** that have an indefinite shape, or that consist of small **crystals** in masses.
- **MATRIX**
The **rock** in which a gem is found. Also known as host or parent rock.
- **METAMICT**
Refers to material that is breaking down from a crystalline to an **amorphous** state, due to the presence of radioactive elements.
- **METAMORPHIC ROCKS**
**Rocks** that have been changed by heat and/or pressure to form new rocks consisting of new **minerals**.
- **MICROCRYSTALLINE**
**Mineral** structure in which **crystals** are too small to be detected by the naked eye.
- **MINERALS**
Inorganic, naturally occurring materials with a constant chemical composition and regular internal atomic structure.

- **MIXED-CUT**
Cut in which the **facets** above and below the **girdle** are styled in different ways – usually **brilliant-cut** above and **step-cut** below.
- **MOHS' SCALE OF HARDNESS**
Measure of a **mineral's** hardness in relation to other minerals, based on its ability to resist scratching.
- **OPALESCENCE**
Milky blue form of **iridescence**.
- **ORE**
**Rock** that contains metals capable of being extracted commercially.
- **ORGANIC GEM**
Gem made by or derived from living organisms.
- **PARTI-COLOURED**
Used to describe single **crystals** made of different coloured parts.
- **PASTE**
Glass made to **imitate** gems.
- **PAVILION**
Lower part of a cut stone, below the **girdle**.
- **PEGMATITE**
An **igneous rock** formed as residual liquids from **magma** cool, often forming large **crystals**.
- **PLACER DEPOSIT**
Concentrated (**secondary**) deposit of minerals, usually in rivers or seas.
- **PLATY**
**Habit** characterized by flat, thin, plate-like **crystals**.
- **PLEOCHROIC**
Term used to describe a gem that appears two or more different colours or shades when viewed from different directions.
- **POLYCRYSTALLINE**
Refers to a **mineral** made of many small **crystals**.
- **PRIMARY DEPOSIT**
Material still in its original **rock**. *See also* **Secondary deposit**.
- **PRISMATIC**
**Habit** in which parallel pairs of rectangular **faces** form prisms.
- **PSEUDOMORPH**
One **mineral** occurring in the crystal shape of another.
- **REFRACTION**
Bending of light as it passes from air into a different medium.
- **REFRACTIVE INDEX (RI)**
Measure of the slowing down and bending of light rays as they enter a **gemstone**. May be used to identify individual gem **species**.
- **REFRACTOMETER**
Apparatus used to measure the **refractive indices** of gems.

- **RHOMB**
Shape rather like a skewed cube.
- **ROCK**
Material made up of one or more **minerals**.
- **ROUGH**
Term used to describe a **rock** or **crystal** still in its natural state, before **faceting** or polishing.
- **SCHILLER/SHEEN**
Form of **iridescence**.
- **SCHIST**
**Metamorphic rock** in which the **crystals** are in parallel arrangement.
- **SECONDARY DEPOSIT**
Gems or **minerals** that have been separated from their original **rock** and re-deposited elsewhere. *See also* **Primary deposit**.
- **SEDIMENTARY ROCKS**
**Rocks** formed by the consolidation and hardening of **rock** fragments, organic remains, or other material.
- **SPECIES**
Used in this book to refer to individual gems that have distinct characteristics which may be defined and verified.
- **SPECIFIC GRAVITY (SG)**
Density, measured as the weight of the material compared with that of an equal volume of water.
- **SPECTROSCOPE**
Instrument used to view the **absorption spectra** of gemstones.
- **STEP-CUT (OR TRAP-CUT)**
Cut characterized by a rectangular **table facet** and **girdle**, with rect-angular facets parallel to these.
- **STONE**
Term used for any **gemstone**.
- **STRIATION**
Parallel scratch, groove, or line.
- **SYMMETRY, AXIS OF**
Imaginary line through a **crystal**. If the crystal were rotated about the axis it would present an identical aspect two or more times in a rotation of 360 degrees.
- **SYNTHETIC GEMSTONE**
Laboratory-made stone whose chemical composition and optical properties are similar to those of its natural equivalent.
- **TABLE FACET**
Central **facet** on a gem's **crown**.
- **TRICHROIC**
Refers to a gem that appears three different colours or shades when viewed from different directions.
- **VITREOUS**
Glass-like (used to describe **lustre**).

# INDEX

# Useful Addresses

**Gemmological Association
of Great Britain**
27 Greville Street, London, EC1N 8TN
www.gagtl.ac.uk

**The National Association of Goldsmiths**
78a Luke Street, London, EC2A 4XG

**British Museum (Natural History)**
Mineralogy Department,
Cromwell Road, London, SW7 5BD
www.nhm.ac.uk

**Royal Museum of Scotland**
Chambers Street, Edinburgh, EH1 1JF
www.nms.ac.uk

**The Gemmological Association of Australia**
PO Box 14008, Melbourne City Mail Centre,
Victoria, 8001, Australia

**Gemological Institute of America**
1660 Stewart Street, Santa Monica,
CA 9040, USA

**American Gem Trade Association**
181 World Trade Center, 2050 Stemmons
Expressway, Dallas, TX 75207, USA
www.agta.org

**The Smithsonian Institute**
Washington DC, 20560, USA
www.si.edu

# Acknowledgments

**The author** would like to thank the Mineralogy Department curatorial team at the Natural History Museum (Alan Hart, David Smith, Peter Tandy, Henry Buckley, Andrew Clark) and the team leader Dr. Robert Symes for their help in getting gem specimens to Harry Taylor in the Photographic Department; my husband, Robert, and daughters, Alice and Emily, for giving me time to work quietly in my study, with only a few interruptions; Dr. Roger Harding, Alan Jobbins, Dr. Joseph Peters, and Christine Woodward for their expert help; and the team at Dorling Kindersley, especially Alison Edmonds, Alison Shackleton, Jonathan Metcalf, Mary-Clare Jerram, Lesley Malkin, and Lucinda Hawksley.

**Dorling Kindersley** would like to thank: Michael Allaby for compiling the index; Caroline Church for the endpapers; Neal Cobourne for the jacket design; Peter Bull for the rock cycle diagram 12 (tr); Janos Marffy for all additional artwork; Julia Pashley for picture research; Harry Taylor for his patience and co-operation during photography; Alastair Wardle for gem diagrams and the map on pp.14–15; Alison Edmonds for the loan of diamond jewellery for photography, 55 (cl); R. Keith Mitchell for the loan of taaffeite for photography 80 (t); Lesley Malkin and Constance Novis for additional editorial assistance; Peter Cross, Ann Thompson, and Kevin Ryan for additional design assistance.

**All specially commissioned photography** by Harry Taylor, except 11 (tr), 12 (cl), 13 (tr), 17 (bl & br), 18 (br), 19 (cl), 21 (cl), 26 (cutting a brilliant), 27 (br), 28 (tl & tr), 33 (tl, tr, bl, & br), 34 (tr, bl, & br), 35 (br), 36 (tl, cl & cr), 48 (c & bl), 50 (t & br), 55 (br), 57 (tl), 60 (br), 63 (tr & br), 67 (bl), 68 (cr), 69 (tr & br), 70 (cr & br), 71 (cl, cr, & br), 72 (cr), 74 (cl), 76 (bc), 77 (cl & cr), 78 (br), 81 (br), 82 (br), 83 (br), 85 (br), 87 (tc), 88 (bl & br), 92 (tr, tl, & bl), 93 (tr & c), 94 (br), 95 (cr & c), 98 (tr), 100 (br), 101 (tcr), 104 (tr), 106 (br), 107 (cr), 109 (tr), 110 (br), 112 (br), 113 (br), 117 (bl), 120 (tl, tr, & cl), 124 (bl), 125 (tr, cl, bl, & br), 130 (cl, cr, & br), 134 (c), 135 (bc), 138 (br), 139 (l), 141 (cl), 142 (bl & br), 143 (tl), 145 (cl, cr, bl, & br), 148 (br) by Colin Keates; 30 (tr) by Dave King; and 144 (t, bl, & br) by Matthew Ward.

**The publishers** would also like to thank the following for permission to reproduce their photographs and illustrations:
Vicky Ambery-Smith 50 (tl); Asprey Ltd 31

(br), 49 (cl); Bridgeman Art Library 57 (tc); Cartier 27 (tr), 29 (tr); Crown Copyright (reproduced by permission of the Controller of Her Majesty's Stationery Office) 7 (tr); De Beers 13 (bl & br), 14 (cl); Garrard, the Crown Jewellers 49 (br), 55 (t); Andrew Farmer 28 (bl); Michael Holford 11 (r), 31 (tr), 32 (c & tr), 59 (tc), 106 (br); The Hutchison Library 8 (br); Alan Jobbins 6 (tr), 8 (c), 15 (tr & bl), 20 (cr), 24 (br), 25 (tl, cr, & br), 32 (cr), 35 (cr), 36 (tr & br), 37 (tr), 56 (tr), 59 (tr), 60 (tr), 62 (tr), 75 (tr & bl), 82 (tr), 86 (bl), 94 (tr & cl), 135 (cr & br), 140 (tr), 145 (tr); Bernd Munsteiner 2, 29 (br); The Natural History Museum 11 (bl), 13 (cr), 21 (br), 23 (tr), 24 (bl), 38 (tl); The Platinum Advisory Centre 26 (br), 53 (tl & br)/Nicolas Sapieha 53 (tr); The Smithsonian Institute 76 (tr), 94 (cr), 107 (tr); Tiffany & Co 51 (tr & br), 55 (cr); The Victoria & Albert Museum 31 (cl), 32 (br), 125 (cr); Werner Forman Archive 30 (cr); The Worshipful Company of Goldsmiths 49 (tr), 50 (bl), 51 (bl & cr), 53 (bl).